THE TASTE OF GLOUCESTER

A Fisherman's Wife Cooks

© Ninth Edition

Written and Compiled by . . .
The Fishermen's Wives of Gloucester
The Cape Ann League of Women Voters

Dedicated to the fishing families of the Gloucester Fleet.

O fish you make a dainty dish
  enriching shore folks lives.
Enjoy fresh fish is our great wish
  for we be fishermen's wives.
We be the women of the men
  who cast their nets at sea
and by their labor, now and then,
  share in its rich bounty.
We be the women who watch the skies
  and tense to the weather reports;
we be the women who pray and rise
  from our knees in the fishing ports.
Cold are the seas and iced our hearts
when the northern gales come down
  when every shriek of the wind imparts
that boats and men can drown.
Yes, fish, you make a dainty dish
  enriching shore folks lives
but it's little we get for the worry and fret
  of being the fishermen's wives.

Yon Swanson

For Additional Copies write:
Taste Of Gloucester
P.O. Box 1181
Gloucester, MA 01930

Table of Contents

The Captains
of the
Gloucester Fleet
1976

St. Joseph	Capt. Peter Lovasco
Lady in Blue	Capt. Sam Frontiero
Ida and Joseph	Capt. Joseph Calomo
Jeanne D'Arc	Capt. Joseph Parco
Holy Family	Capt. Carlo Moceri
Holy Cross	Capt. Sam Lovasco
Joseph and Lucia	Capt. Gaetano Brancelone
Santa Lucia	Capt. Paul Brancelone
St. Peter	Capt. Joseph Giacalone
St. Peter III	Capt. Tommy Favazza
Vincie N.	Capt. Salvatore Novello
Bonaventure	Capt. Nicolas Novello
Curlew	Capt. Dominic Montagnino
Teresa R.	Capt. Gus Sanfilippo
St. George	Capt. Antonio Sanfillippo
Vincie and Josephine	Capt. Salvatore Ferrara
Acme	Capt. John Cusumano
Serafina II	Capt. Benjamin Chiancola
Judith Lee Rose	Capt. Frank Rose
Padre Pio I	Capt. John Sanfilippo
Katie D.	Capt. Vito Ciaramitaro
Gaetano S.	Capt. Joe Parisi
Odessa	Capt. Eric Nielsen
Invader	Capt. Hilary Dombrowski
Mabel Susan	Capt. Bob Anderson
Lady Rose	Capt. Joe Agrusso
Peggy Bell	Capt. Bill Sibley
Debbie Rose	Capt. John Randazza
Salvatore P	Capt. James Parisi
Salvatore and Grace	Capt. Samuel Frontiero
Mary Ann	Capt. Mike Diliberti
Mother and Grace	Capt. Sebastian Moceri
American Eagle	Capt. Joseph Piscitello
Anna Maria	Capt. Stephen Demetri
Little Flower	Capt. Vito Ferrara
Spray	Capt. Joseph Saputo
Agatha and Patricia	Capt. Charles Parisi
Tina Marie	Capt. John Quince
Joseph & Lucia II	Capt. Nino Branceleone
Antonina	Capt. Santo Mineo
Anthony & Josephine	Capt. Vito Favaloro

The Captains of the Gloucester Fleet 2012

	F/V		F/V
Capt. Bonnie Akerly	Explorer II	Capt. Matteo Logrande	Little Sandra
Capt. Thomas Bartlett	Marilyn Louise	Capt. Thomas Lupo	Jennie C
Capt. Carl Bouchard	Stormy Weather	Capt. Paul Metivier	Debra Ann II
Capt. Busty Brancaleone	Tina & Tom	Capt. Peter Mondello	Allison Carol
Capt. B.G. Brown	Kathryn Leigh	Capt. John Montgomery	Chandelle
Capt. William Brown	Beacon	Capt. Daniel Murphy	Bantry Bay
Capt. Daniel Bubb	Belinda B	Capt. Stephanie Noto	Grace Marie
	Melissa Sue	Capt. Sam Novello	Capt. Novello
Capt. Corrado Buccheri	Horizon, Irmac II	Capt. Dennis Oconnel	Lady Elaine
Capt. Richard Burgess	Blue Fin Singer	Capt. Joseph Orlando	Padre Pio
	Bureaucracy	Capt. Joe Palazzolo	Franseca & Carlo
	Heidi & Heather	Capt. Craig Porter	Kenneth J. Duncan
	Hollywood II		Manford L. Porter
	Julie Ann	Capt. Philip Powell	Foxy Lady
	Red Tape		Lowe
	Ryan Zachary		Solina Soo
	Scotia Boat Too	Capt. Joe Randazzo	Razzo
	Starcraft	Capt. Dennis Robillard	Julie Ann II
Capt. Mark Byard	SS Melon III	Capt. Vincenzo Russo	Mary and Josephine
Capt. Mark Carnevale	Carol Ann		Miss Trish II
Capt. Mark Carroll	Harvest Moon	Capt. Clark Sandler	Sea Farmer II
Capt. Christian Chadwick	1988 Sea Nymph	Capt. Accursio Sanfilippo	Captain Dominic
	Native Son	Capt. Gus Sanfilippo	Lily Jean
Capt. Paul Cohan	Sasquatch III	Capt. Ignazio Sanfilippo	Cat Eyes
Capt. Daniel Connors	Early Times	Capt. Joseph Sanfilippo	Maria G.S.
Capt. Matthew Cooney	Miss Meredith	Capt. Sal Sanfilippo	Janaya & Joseph
Capt. Al Cottone	Sabrina Maria	Capt. Jim Santapaola	Amanda & Andy
Capt. Wm. Cunningham	Fair Wind		Amanda & Andy II
Capt. Mark Davis	Mackerel		Amanda Leigh
Capt. Joe Dimaio	Princess Laura		Lowe
	Princess Elena		W M F
Capt. John Dinuccio	Lisa-Rose	Capt. Jon Savage	Andromeda
Capt. Daniel Dunbar	Little Mako	Capt. Arthur Sawyer	Miss Carla
Capt. Lance Edwards	Catherine M	Capt. Frank Sciortino	Christina Eleni
Capt. Peter Fadden	Becky and Ben	Capt. Russel Sherman	Lady Jane
	Catherine F	Capt. William Skrobacz	Toots
	Rebecca Anne	Capt. Edward Smith	Ambjorg & Julie
Capt. Jim Ford	Lisa Ann II		Brittannika I
Capt. Peter Fyrberg	Merganser		Brittannika II
Capt. Douglas Germain	Labor in Vain		Cape Dory
Capt. Nino Giacalone	Caterina G		Claudia Marie
Capt. Vito Giacalone	Jenny G	Capt. Russell P. Stribley	Sally & Katherine
Capt. John Greenleaf	David and Jenna	Capt. Scott Swicker	Aaron & Alexa
	David and Jenna II		Ashley & Anthony
Capt. Darren Hart	Comet	Capt. Vincenzo Taormina	Miss Sandy
Capt. Brian Higgins	Toby Ann	Capt. Thomas Testaverde	Midnight Sun
Capt. Thomas Hill	K + S	Capt. Paul Theriault	Terminator
	Karoline Marie	Capt. Jeffery Tutein	Lucky Strike
	Stephanie Lynn	Capt. Jay Vanderpool	Alyssa & Andrew
Capt. Dean Holt	Katie Mae	Capt. Paul Vitale	Angela & Rose
Capt. Joseph Jurek	Mystique Lady	Capt. Steve Wojcicki	Kristine Marie
Capt. Peter Libro	Cabaret IV		
	Dolores		
	Sea Skiff		
	Skiff II		

The Man at the Wheel

Sculpture by Leonard Craske
Stacy Boulevard, Gloucester, MA
Dedicated 1925

Introduction

The statue of the "Man at the Wheel" looks out over the Harbor in the historic port of Gloucester, Massachusetts. It symbolizes the courage and steadfastness of "they who go down to the sea in ships", the men who fish out of Gloucester.

Though the days are gone of the high-masted schooners which originally made Gloucester famous, the city is still a working fishing port, unique for its spirit of community. Not only Gloucester's fishermen, but also her poets, her artists and craftsmen, her industries and her cuisine all reflect her continuing ties with the sea.

Gloucester seafood has long enjoyed a nationwide following. Visitors to the area invariably sample the fare at traditional waterfront restaurants. Countless others buy fish products such as fresh and frozen fish fillets and fish sticks from Gloucester-based leaders of the fish processing industry.

However, some of the most exciting fish cookery in Gloucester has been unavailable to the general public. Much of the local fish is prepared and served in the homes of the fishermen themselves by ingenious cooks like Lena Novello, who are constantly creating new ways to serve the products that their families catch.

The fishing families of Gloucester come from many backgrounds.: Italian, Portugese, Scandinavian, and New England Yankee, and have a tremendous variety of Atlantic seafood to use: cod, haddock, flounder, pollock and cusk, lobsters, shrimp, clams and scallops. They have elevated fish preparation from the standard broil or fry methods to a separate cuisine of amazingly unique dishes.

Now the fishermen's wives have agreed to share their culinary secrets in this cookbook. Some of these recipes have been passed down through the generations; others were created to use new fish products. All will provide the average cook with a new confidence in cooking fish and a greater appreciation for seafood. In addition to the recipes, information has been included about the selection, buying, cleaning, and filleting of fish to insure perfect reproduction of Gloucester cuisine in kitchens throughout the country. Cooks of all caliber should appreciate the opportunity to serve an often unrecognized source of good taste and nutrition.

For the fishermen's wives, the chance to share their knowledge of cooking fish brings more than personal satisfaction. The promotion of seafood guarantees the livelihood of their families by ensuring that the boats will continue to find markets for their catch. The survival of the great seafaring traditions of Gloucester depends on the ability of these home kitchen "experts" to transmit the excitement and ease of cooking with "The Taste of Gloucester".

THE
WORKING
HARBOR 1976

I was not born there, came, as so many of the people came,
from elsewhere. That is, my father did. And not from the provinces,
not from Newfoundland. But we came early enough. When he came,
there were three hundred sail could fill the harbor,
if they were all in, as for the races, say
Or as now the Italians are in, for San Pietro,
and the way it is from Town Landing, all band-concert, and fireworks.

So I answered her: Yes,
I knew (I had that to compare to it, was Worcester)

As the people of the earth are now, Gloucester is heterogeneous,
and so can know polis

so few
have the polis
in their eye

        The brilliant Portuguese owners, they do. They pour the money
        back into engines, into their ships, whole families do, put it back
        in. They are but extensions of their own careers as mastheadsmen -
        as Burkes....

So few need to,
to make the many
share (to have it, too)

but those few...
            What kills me is, how do these others think the eyes are
            sharp? by gift? bah by love of self?
            try it by God? ask the bean sandwich

There are no hierarchies, no infinite, no such many as mass, there
are only eyes in all heads, to be looked out of

The Maximus Poems, I, II, III, Charles Olson

A Note on Charles Olson
  *Charles Olson (1910-1970) was born and raised in Gloucester
and spent most of his later years there writing. The above is a
selection from his* Maximus Poems, *which he himself chose for use
by the Fishermen's Wives in a cookbook.*

All About Fish

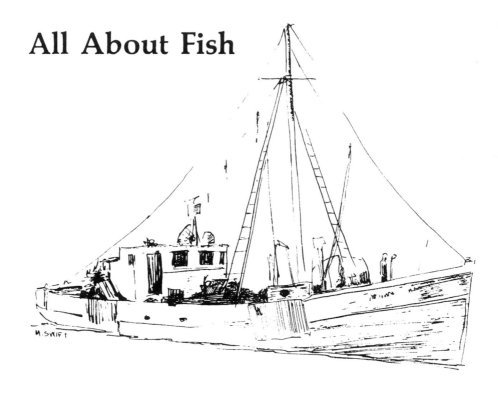

M.SWIFT

Fish is a high-quality protein food which is also very low in carbohydrates. It is, therefore, an excellent alternative to meat. Many of the fin fish are low in fat values. Among the least fat fish are bass, perch, flounder, trout, haddock and cod. Those that contain the most fat are salmon, catfish, mackerel, bluefish, herring, shad, sturgeon, tuna and red snapper. Fish is also an excellent source of minerals, including iodine and other trace elements.

SELECTING AND CARING FOR FISH

Fresh fish, or fish that was frozen while fresh, has full or bulging bright eyes, bright red gills, firm and elastic flesh and no smell. Be sure the flesh along the backbone smells fresh; it spoils there first. Also if fish is pinkish it has started to spoil. Fresh fish sinks in fresh water. If it floats, it should not be used.

As soon as fish comes from the market, clean it and wipe dry with paper towels. Keep fish refrigerated until ready to use. Fish that is cleaned and frozen immediately after it is caught and is kept frozen until needed does not lose its flavor. To thaw place in refrigerator overnight.

AMOUNT OF FISH TO BUY

If the fish bought is filleted, one-third of a pound should be allowed for each person. If fish is bought in the round (with bones, head, tail, etc.) at least one-half pound must be bought for each person.

8

Forms of Fish

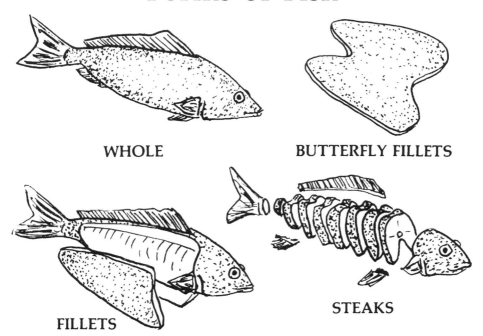

WHOLE

BUTTERFLY FILLETS

FILLETS

STEAKS

HOW TO CLEAN AND FILLET FISH

Put fish on bread board or flat firm surface, dark side up. Make sure your knife is sharp. Make a slit in the skin right above the tail, perpendicular to the backbone (or middlebone, the one that runs down the center). Sprinkle the slit with salt and leave it a few minutes. The salt will loosen the skin right near the cut, so you can get a grip on it. Hold the fish firmly by the tail with one hand and pull the skin off with the other. Proceed slowly and if your fish is sticking, put a weight on the tail and use the liberated hand to hold the knife. Pull and cut simultaneously, freeing the flesh as you peel back the skin.

There are two fillets on each side of the backbone, four little ones instead of two big. Cut a slit to the bone down the center line of the skinned fish. Angle the knife against the bone, as close to parallel as possible, and slice carefully outward, lifting off the fillet. Do the other side the same way. Cut the backbone out from above and separate the bottom skins off with the knife, because these fillets are thinner than the top ones and they usually tear if you try to pull them. Use a scraping motion, pressing down against the skin with the knife blade.

This whole process is much easier than it sounds. It has three advantages — you can tell the freshness of a whole fish much more easily, you get the bones and trimmings to make broth for sauce or chowder, and you pay less for your fish.

9

WINE WITH FISH

There is a French saying, "Poisson sans vin est poison" and while it is unlikely that anyone was ever poisoned by eating fish without wine, a good bottle of wine does add to the enjoyment of carefully prepared seafood.

A light dry white wine is usually considered to be most suitable. The Chablis and Rhine wines are very good examples, served chilled, or course. A chilled Moselle-type or a Muscadet is also excellent. If you prefer red wines, a well-chilled rose goes very well with seafood. It is strictly a matter of preference; however the wine should be a light one so as not to overpower the delicate flavor of the fish.

ABOUT THIS BOOK

Many of the recipes on the following pages call for a specific type of fish. Because of the regional and seasonal variations some substitutions may be necessary. Other recipes require "any white fillet." The descriptions of North Atlantic fish on pages 11-12 may be helpful in selecting the appropriate type of fish. In all cases, when in doubt, consult your local fish market. The index beginning on page 92 lists dishes using specific varieties of seafood, so that the readers can select a recipe based on the kind of fish which is available to them.

FISH FROM OUR FLEET

SWORDFISH

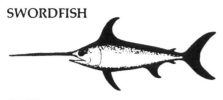

Cut into steaks, delicious broiled, seasonal summer fish.

BASS

Not caught except by sport fishermen on Cape Ann in summer months, but available year-round in other states. Best broiled or baked whole and stuffed.

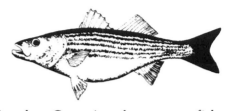

BLUEFISH

Another Cape Ann large sport fish, very vicious when alive, served baked and stuffed, a dark moist meat. This should not be confused with Boston bluefish or pollock.

POLLOCK

Also known as Boston bluefish, a dark meat sold in thick fillets. It turns lighter when cooked. It is found year round and is usually a less expensive fish.

COD

Available year-round. Fish that Gloucester was originally famous for, dried and salted. Now all purpose white fillets.

HADDOCK

Year round fish. Number one choice in white fish. Filleted, used baked and stuffed, fried, poached. Best chowder fish. Best known species of fish in New England, but becoming very expensive.

MACKEREL

Dark-fleshed fish, rich in fats. Particularly delicious served split and barbequed.

FLOUNDER

Caught year round. Many species. Most common North Atlantic catches yellowtails or blackbacks. Usually served filleted and deep-fried.

SOLE

The king of flounders. Delicate, extra-white meat. Prepared baked or fried.

HAKE

A softer fish. Excellent for fish cakes and cutlets, baked or fried. Try it corned.

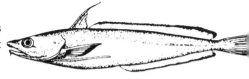

WHITING

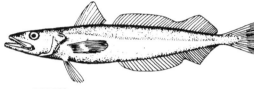

White soft delicate meat. Served fried or baked when filleted or in soup. Also known as silver hake.

CUSK

White fish served filleted and baked or fried. Blander taste than haddock and needs seasoning or a sauce.

SCROD OR SCHROD Small haddock or cod.

HALIBUT

A white meat fish usually as steaks, broiled or baked. The species is becoming rare in the North Atlantic and expensive in the market.

OCEAN PERCH

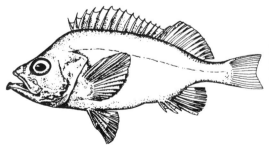

Also called redfish, is gaining in popularity. Distinctive pink colored meat - lean and clean.

MORE FOOD FROM THE FLEET

EEL

A high concentration of protein is found in the nutritious eel. A new easier method for skinning eels is to put them first under the broiler, turning to expose all parts of the skin to the high heat. Then peel off the skin, and cut in chunks.

SQUID

Italian cooks have long sung the praises of the delicious "Calamari," with its chewy texture and sweet rich flavor. Now this unusual seafood is gaining wider acceptance.

DOGFISH

Although it is considered a "nuisance fish" for local fisherman, new methods of skinning the spiny dogfish may soon make it as readily available here as in Europe. Marinate the dogfish steaks for several hours or overnight and fry or broil as with halibut.

MONKFISH

Monkfish or "poor man's lobster" is a reasonably priced fish with a taste and texture quite like the more expensive lobster. The large tail of the monkfish, the only part used, is usually sold as fish steaks. These steaks may be cut into small chunks and used in any of the scallop recipes.

RECIPES

APPETIZERS

TINY COCKTAIL FISH PUFFS

2 lbs. skinless fillets of whiting,
cod, or haddock, thawed if frozen
1 large onion, quartered
½ lb. fresh pork fat
3 eggs

¼ cup flour
½ teaspoon grated nutmeg
1½ teaspoons salt
¼ teaspoon white pepper
½ to 3/4 cup carbonated water
butter

Put fish, then onion and pork fat through fine blade of food grinder or into blender until smooth but not mushy. Place in a large bowl. Beat in eggs one at a time with electric beater. Beat in flour, nutmeg, salt, and pepper, continue beating while adding the carbonated water, until mixture is bubbly and light. Cover; refrigerate about 2 hours.

Shape into tiny balls with two tablespoons dipped in cold water, using about 1 rounded tablespoon for each. Saute fish in ¼ to ½ inch of hot butter in a large skillet. Spoon them fairly close together; cook about 7 to 8 minutes on each side or until crisp and golden brown, turning several times. Drain on paper towel.

SEA FOOD CANAPES

3 slices of white bread
    trimmed and sliced in half
6 large sardines or
6 tablespoons lobster or
    other sea food chopped fine
Juice of 1 lemon

Salt
Worcestershire sauce
Pickled beets
6 large olives
lemon slices for garnish

Remove skin and backbone and flake the sardines with a fork. Or chop cooked lobster meat very fine. Season with lemon juice, salt, and a few drops of Worcestershire sauce. Spread the bread with the mixture and decorate by placing in the center of each canape a small circle of pickled beet. Cut a slice from the end of a large olive so that it will stand firmly and place this in the center of the beet.
Garnish serving tray with thin slices of lemon.

BROILED SCALLOPS HAWAIIAN

24 small scallops
24 pineapple wedges

24 (4-inch) strips bacon
6 slices buttered toast cut
into 2 inch squares

Place a scallop and a pineapple wedge at opposite ends of each bacon strip. Roll trips toward the center so the scallops and pineapple are wrapped in bacon. Secure with toothpick. Broil until bacon is crisp, about 10 minutes, turning to brown all sides. Place with toothpick end in square of bread.

GLOUCESTER SEA PUFFS
40 strip pieces

1½ pounds fish fillets (flounder, pollock, haddock, or any white fish)
2¼ cups self-rising flour
2 tablespoons chopped parsley

2 cloves minced garlic
3 medium eggs
½ teaspoon black pepper
1¼ cup milk
4 cups vegetable oil for frying

Cut fish into 5 inch strips, ¼ to ½ inch thick. Season lightly with salt and set aside. Beat eggs well, add milk and mix well. Combine flour, parsley, garlic and pepper. Add to egg and milk mixture. Mix well. If batter is too thick add a little more milk. Heat oil to boiling point in heavy pan or dutch oven. Dip fish pieces in batter until they are well covered. It may help to stir with a large spoon. Brown pieces in oil. They will float. Turn them over to brown evenly. Drain on paper towels. Puffs can be frozen and then reheated in hot oven.

SEA SCALLOP COCKTAIL
Serves Six

2 pounds sea scallops
1 cup mayonnaise
½ cup dairy sour cream
3 tablespoons minced onion
1 tablespoon prepared horseradish

dash tabasco sauce
2 teaspoons prepared mustard
3 tablespoons minced sweet gherkins
3 tablespoons minced stuffed olives

Cut large scallops in half; cook in simmering salted water 3 to 5 minutes (after water returns to simmer). Do not overcook. Drain. Chill. Combine remaining ingredients; chill; serve as cocktail sauce with scallops.

16

SHRIMP DIP

Blend together:
8 ounces cream cheese   8 tablespoons mayonnaise
Mix in:
2 tablespoons Worcestershire sauce   ½ pound cut-up cooked native shrimp
2 tablespoons onion juice   1 teaspoon red horseradish (if desired)
2 diced fresh tomatoes

Refrigerate. Serve with crackers or chips.
Crabmeat or lobster may be substituted for shrimp.

LOBSTER WHIP

½ pound lobster meat
1 eight-ounce package cream
   cheese, softened
2 tablespoons sour cream
1 small onion minced
¼ cup slivered almonds

salt, pepper, celery salt,
2 dashes of Worcestershire
   sauce

Place all ingredients in blender or food processor. Mix well. Pour into 1 pint
oven dish. Sprinkle with slivered almonds. Heat in 375° oven for 15 minutes.
Serve on crackers directly from oven dish.

LILLY'S FAVORITE FISH DIP
Makes 3 cups dip

1 pound pollock or cusk fillets,
   fresh or frozen
2 cups water
1 stalk celery, cut in 4 pieces
1 bay leaf
3/4 teaspoon salt

½ cup salad dressing or
   mayonnaise
½ cup Russian dressing
   (pouring type)
½ cup finely chopped celery
¼ cup finely chopped red onion
paprika

Thaw frozen fish. Place water, celery, bay leaf and salt in saucepan. Bring to
boil. Add fish; cover and simmer until fish flakes easily when tested with a
fork, about 10 minutes. Chill; skin and flake fish. Combine fish, dressing,
celery and onion; mix well. Sprinkle with paprika. Serve with crackers or
potato chips.

LOBSTER PUFFS

1 pound lobster meat,   lemon juice to taste
  fresh or frozen   mayonnaise to hold mixture together
1 scallion, minced fine   ¼ cup chopped celery

Drain lobster and chop well. Mix all ingredients together for filling. Make tiny cream puffs or buy in package. Fill each puff with lobster mixture.
Also makes an excellent sandwich filling.

FISHWICHES

1 cup cooked, flaked fish   ¼ cup mayonnaise
  (Boston Bluefish or Haddock) 2 tablespoons catchup
¼ cup chopped celery   salt and pepper to taste
1 teaspoon chopped parsley

Great for appetizing sandwich fillings. Mix all these ingredients together. Season to taste and spread between slices of bread. Can also be served on crackers.

FISH SALAD WITH DILL

This salad can be made with poached halibut or shrimp or a combination of both, as below.

2 stalks celery with leaves   1½ pounds small shrimp in shells
2 slices lemon   2 teaspoons lemon juice
10 peppercorns   2 tablespoons minced fresh dill
1 tablespoon salt   ¼ cup mayonnaise
2 pounds halibut fillets

Bring 2 or 3 quarts water to boiling in two large saucepans. Add 1 stalk celery, 1 slice lemon, 5 peppercorns and 1½ teaspoons salt to each pan. Poach halibut in one pan for about 8 minutes and shrimp in the other for 6 to 8 minutes or until tender. Remove and drain both.
Remove any bones and skin from halibut. Peel and de-vein shrimp. Break halibut into small pieces. Shrimp can be cut in half, if desired. Combine shrimp and fish in a large bowl; sprinkle with lemon juice and dill. Add mayonnaise and fold gently to combine. Taste; add additional salt and pepper, if you wish. Chill several hours or until quite cold. Serve on Bibb or Boston lettuce.

SAVORY FISH SALAD

1½ pounds Boston Bluefish (pollock) fillets or other fish fillets, fresh or frozen
3 hard-cooked eggs, chopped
2 tablespoons sweet pickle relish drained
1/8 teaspoon pepper
3/4 cup mayonnaise

3 cups diced celery
¼ cup green pepper, diced
3/4 cup cooked peas
¼ teaspoon salt
1 tablespoon lemon juice
several dashes liquid hot pepper sauce
marinade

Marinade : Combine 1 cup seasoned French dressing, ¼ cup lemon juice or vinegar, 2 tablespoons salad oil, 1 teaspoon soy sauce, 1 teaspoon dill weed.

Thaw fish. Poach fillets until fork tender in water to cover. Drain. Pour marinade over hot fillets. Let stand several hours, or until cold. Turn fillets several times during standing period. Cube cold fillets. Add remaining ingredients and toss to mix. Serve in lettuce cups, or shredded lettuce with extra dressing and a slice of lemon.
Serve with tomato and cucumber slices and hot biscuits with butter or crisp toasted crackers and relish tray.

FILLET OF SOLE QUICKIES

Fillet of sole slices
½ cup milk
1 egg
½ teaspoon salt

Seasoned Italian bread crumbs
lemon slices
chopped parsley

Beat together milk, egg, and salt. Dip slices of sole in milk and egg mixture, then roll in seasoned Italian bread crumbs. Place in baking dish. Bake at 475° for 15 minutes. Garnish with thin slices of lemon dipped in chopped parsley. Serve with tartar sauce.

FISH STICKS ON A RAFT

Great for cooking in toaster oven. Serves 1 person.

1 slice Italian bread
4-5 tablespoons grated Provolone cheese
3 fish sticks, frozen

1 tablespoon finely minced onion
2 tablespoons tomato sauce
oregano

Sprinkle slice of bread with 2 tablespoons Provolone cheese. Place fish sticks on top of cheese, then sprinkle with onion. Put 2 tablespoons of cheese on top of onion and cover with strained tomato. Sprinkle with oregano. Top with remaining cheese. Wrap in tinfoil and bake 350°F 15-20 minutes.

HADDOCK QUICHES
Serves 6

1½ pounds boiled and flaked
   haddock
¼ pound grated Swiss cheese
6 individual pie shells
4 eggs
2 cups light cream

1 teaspoon grated onion
1 teaspoon salt
½ teaspoon nutmeg
1 tablespoon minced green pepper
dash of pepper
¼ cup sherry

Flake haddock and toss in cheese. Place in bottom of pie shells. Combine 4 eggs, cream, Sherry, onion, green pepper, and seasoning. Beat together until well blended. Pour over haddock and cheese mixture. Bake at 425° for 15 minutes. Reduce heat to 325° and bake 15 minutes more.

THE JOHN DORY
Makes 36 to 40

1½ pounds ocean perch, whiting,
   or other fish fillets, fresh or frozen
1½ teaspoons salt
Hot water
¼ cup margarine or cooking oil
2 cups chopped celery
1 cup chopped onion

1 cup shredded raw potato
1 can (10 ounce) tomatoes,
   undrained
1 teaspoon oregano
¼ teaspoon pepper
¼ cup grated Romano cheese
Crust

Crust

Cut 6 tablespoons shortening into 6 cups self-rising flour. Add cold water as needed (about 2 cups) to make a stiff dough.

Thaw frozen fish. Combine fish and 3/4 teaspoon salt in deep skillet or Dutch oven. Add hot water to cover. Simmer about 10 minutes or until fish flakes easily when tested with a fork. Drain fish and chill. Remove skin from fish and flake. Heat margarine or cooking oil in skillet; add celery and onion and cook until almost tender, 7 to 10 minutes. Add potato and cook 5 minutes. Add tomatoes, oregano, remaining 3/4 teaspoon salt, and pepper. Cook slowly, stirring constantly, about 10 minutes. Chill. Fold in flaked fish and cheese.

Prepare crust while fish mixture is chilling. Divide crust into 4 equal portions. Roll one portion at a time on a lightly floured surface, rolling dough very thin. Cut dough into 4-½ or 5-inch squares. Place 2 tablespoons of fish mixture slightly to one side of center on each square. Moisten edges of squares with water; fold in half and seal edges with tines of fork dipped in flour. Fry in hot oil, 375°F., about 2 minutes or until well browned, turning once. Remove from oil; drain on paper toweling. Serve hot or cold.

SOUPS

FISH STOCK
3 pints

2 pounds fish trimmings
(heads, bones, tails)
2 quarts water
1 bay leaf

2 stalks celery
1 carrot
3 whole peppercorns

Wash trimmings in salted water. Pour water in deep saucepan; add trimmings and spices. Cover tightly and simmer for forty-five minutes. Use as directed.

OLD SALT'S FISH CHOWDER

2 pounds cusk and hake
1 large onion (cut in tiny pieces)
4 slices salt pork
5 potatoes peeled and chopped small

1 pint milk
2 tablespoons butter
2 cups water
salt and pepper to taste

Saute onion and salt pork. Remove pork. Add water, potatoes, and boil for five minutes, add fish which has been cut up in one inch pieces. Boil until potatoes are done. Add milk and butter. Season to taste. Bring to a scald and serve with crackers.

BOUILLABAISSE
8 Servings

1 pound cod fillets
1 pound whiting fillets
1 pound Boston Blue Fish (pollock)
1 pound sea scallops
2 lobsters (boiled separately)
12 mussels (optional)
1 large garlic clove, minced
2 cups of water
salt and pepper

1 large bay leaf
½ teaspoon saffron
1 small can mushrooms
⅓ cup of butter
2 cups canned clam broth
1 cup chopped onion
1 cup sliced celery
2 (1 pound) cans of crushed tomatoes

Cut cod, whiting and bluefish into two inch pieces. Saute onion, celery and garlic in butter. (Do not overcook) Add tomatoes, water, clam broth, mushrooms, herbs, and fish. Bring to a boil; simmer 10 minutes. Add mussels and scallops; simmer ten minutes longer. Season to taste. Crack cooked lobster claws. Remove meat from lobster tail; dice. Add to soup; simmer ten minutes more and serve.

CLAM CHOWDER, NEW ENGLAND STYLE
Serves 4.

1 strip bacon, diced
¼ cup diced onions
2 cans minced clams*
1 cup milk

⅓ cup water
3/4 cup diced potatoes
½ teaspoon salt

Brown bacon in saucepan. Reserve. Drain excess fat. Cook onions 3 minutes. Add liquid from cans of minced clams. Cook until potatoes are soft, 10 minutes. Add 1 cup milk and clams. Heat gently. Add bacon and pat butter to each bowl.
*or 6 fresh cherry stone clams, reserving juice.

FISH CHOWDER
Serves 6

2 pounds cusk, haddock or other fish
3 onions, diced
4 cups diced raw potatoes
1 can evaporated milk

3 cups fresh milk
½ pound margarine
¼ teaspoon pepper
¼ teaspoon savory (optional)
Paprika

Cook onions and potatoes in 2 cups water until almost cooked. Add fish and complete cooking. When fish flakes easily, add butter, salt, pepper, savory and all the milk. Heat completely without boiling. Sprinkle with paprika and let set for 15 minutes.

NORTH ATLANTIC SHRIMP CHOWDER

1½ pounds North Atlantic Shrimp,
  heads off, but shell still on.
1 teaspoon whole allspice
4 tablespoons olive oil
6 cups water
3 cups water
1 cup celery, diced

½ cup onion, diced
1 cup carrots, sliced
1 small, ripe tomato or 2 tablespoons
  canned tomatoes
½ cup frozen peas
1 cup diced potatoes
1 cup tiny macaroni, (cooked
  according to the package)

Tie allspice in cheesecloth and add to the 6 cups of water along with olive oil. Boil for 10 minutes, then add shrimp and wait until the shrimp curls (3 to 5 minutes. Remove shrimp from broth. Set shrimp aside to cool, then peel. Discard spice bag. Add the 3 cups water to stock and bring to a boil; add celery, onions, carrots and tomato. Simmer 10 minutes. Then add peas and diced potatoes. When potatoes are just about cooked, add the cooked drained macaroni along with shrimp.

AGHOITTA a la NOVELLO
(Stew with Fish Croquettes) Serves 6.

1½ pounds raw hake or other
    white fish, (ground up)
1 cup bread crumbs
¼ cup Romano cheese
2 cloves garlic (finely minced)
1 tablespoon chopped parsley
3 eggs, well beaten
1 teaspoon salt
½ teaspoon black pepper

3 tablespoons olive oil
½ cup onion
1 large can stewed tomatoes
4 large potatoes (cut in fours)
1 small can peas
1 cup water
Salt
Pepper

Combine fish, bread crumbs, cheese, garlic, parsley, eggs, salt and pepper. Mix well and shape into croquettes. Heat oil in heavy fry pan; add fish croquettes; brown on both sides and remove from pan. Set aside. Heat 3 tablespoons olive oil in pot or Dutch oven. Saute onion until soft; add tomatoes and water. Cook over medium heat for 15 minutes. Add potatoes; cook 5 more minutes. Add fish croquettes, peas and enough water to cover croquettes. Cook about 15 minutes or until potatoes are done. Salt and pepper to taste.

CIOPPINO
Serves 8

1 large onion, chopped (1 cup)
1 medium-sized green pepper,
    halved, seeded and chopped
½ cup sliced celery
1 carrot, pared and shredded
3 cloves of garlic, minced
3 tablespoons olive oil
2 cans (1 pound each) tomatoes
1 can (8 ounces) tomato sauce
1 teaspoon leaf basil, crumbled
1 bay leaf

1 teaspoon salt
¼ teaspoon pepper
1 pound swordfish steak or
    halibut steak
1 dozen mussels or
1 can (10 ounces) clams in shells
1½ cups dry white wine
1 package (8 ounces) frozen,
    shelled, deveined shrimp
½ pound scallops
2 tablespoons minced parsley

Saute onion, green pepper, celery, carrot and garlic in olive oil until soft in a kettle or Dutch oven. Stir in tomatoes, tomato sauce, basil, bay leaf, salt and pepper. Heat to boiling, reduce heat, cover and simmer 2 hours. Discard bay leaf. While sauce simmers, remove the skin from swordfish or halibut. Cut fish into serving-size pieces. Thoroughly clean mussels or clams. Stir wine into sauce in kettle. Add swordfish, shrimp and scallops. Simmer, covered, 10 minutes longer. Place mussels or clams in a layer on top of fish in kettle; cover; steam 5 to 10 minutes, or until the shells are fully opened and fish flakes easily. Ladle into soup plates or bowls. Sprinkle with parsley. Serve with crusty French or Italian bread.

LOBSTER BISQUE
Serves 2

1 can (6½ ounces) lobster meat
1 can condensed
  cream of asparagus soup
1 can condensed
  cream of mushroom soup
1 cup light cream

Few grains cayenne pepper
2 tablespoons sherry
2 tablespoons minced chives
Parmesan cheese croutons

Blend together soups, cream, lobster and cayenne and bring to a simmering point. When mixture is hot, stir in sherry. Serve with sprinkling of chives and Parmesan cheese croutons.

JEFFREY'S LEDGE CHOWDER

2½ pounds whole fish, haddock or
  whiting, or 2 pounds fillets
6 cups water
1 teaspoon whole allspice in
  cheesecloth
¼ cup olive oil
1 tablespoon chopped parsley

3/4 cup chopped onion
1½ cup diced potato
1 cup small shell macaroni, cooked
1 small ripe tomato or 2
  tablespoons canned tomato
salt and pepper to taste
1 cup celery cut in pieces

Fillet fish and keep body for stock.

Boil water, oil and spice bag in saucepan, 5 minutes, then add fish body and cook 7-10 minutes more. Strain out fish body. Add celery, onions, parsley and tomato to fish stock. When celery is half-cooked, add potato. When potatoes are almost done, add fillets and cook 10 minutes more; add macaroni and bring to boil. (If fillets are used instead of whole fish, follow same instructions omitting whole fish directions. Fish parts simply add flavor.)

QUICK & EASY SUPPER SOUP
Serves 4

½ cup sliced carrots
½ cup water
1 can (10 ounces) frozen condensed
  oyster stew
1 cup cooked halibut or other
  white fish
Dash pepper

½ cup sliced celery
1 can (10 ¼ ounces) frozen clam
  chowder (New England Style)
1½ soup cans milk
½ cup cooked shrimp
Chopped parsley

In covered saucepan, cook carrots and celery in water until just tender. Add soups and milk. Cook over low heat until soup is thawed; stir now and then. Add fish, shrimp and pepper. Heat; do not boil. Garnish with parsley.

CASSEROLES

BOSTON BLUEFISH CASSEROLE
Serves 6

1½ pounds Boston Bluefish (pollock) ¼ pound dry noodles
   fillets or other fish fillets,   2 tablespoons butter
   fresh or frozen   2 tablespoons flour
3 cups milk   1/8 teaspoon pepper
½ teaspoon salt   ¼ teaspoon paprika
¼ pound cheese, grated   ½ teaspoon Worcestershire sauce
1 tablespoon lemon juice   2 cups soft bread crumbs

Thaw fish. Cook fish in salted water 15 minutes. Drain and flake. Cook noodles until tender. Drain. Make white sauce, using half the cheese and Worcestershire sauce and lemon juice. Combine with flaked fish and drained noodles. Pour into 9 x 11 x 2½" pan. Combine remaining cheese and crumbs; sprinkle over top. Bake in slow oven 325°F. for 1 hour. Serve with crisp salad and French bread or marinated vegetables and crusty rolls.

JUBILEE GUMBO
Make your Jubilee "catch" at the market, using fresh fish.

Ocean fish fillets (for example   Olive oil
snapper, cod and sole)   Water
Assorted seafoods (for example, White wine
shrimp, crab and clams)   Salt
Canned tomatoes   Hot pepper sauce
Chopped green pepper   Onion

Combine canned tomatoes with chopped green pepper, onion, olive oil in a deep sauce pan. Simmer until tender. Add water and white wine (half and half) to just cover vegetables with fillets of ocean fish (snapper, cod and sole) and assorted seafoods, the greater the variety the better. Season with salt and hot pepper sauce. Cover and steam approximately 15 minutes. Serve in soup plates over a mound of fluffy rice.

POLLOCK AND SHRIMP DI GLOUCESTER
Serves 8 - 10

2 pounds pollock or cod fillets
fresh or frozen
½ cup chopped onion
¼ cup olive or cooking oil
2 teaspoons salt
¼ teaspoon pepper
2 cups water
1 can (12 ounces) tomato paste
2 cups small shrimp, cleaned and
deveined (about ½ pound.)

1-10 ounce package frozen
mixed vegetables, thawed
½ cup sliced pitted black
olives, optional
2 tablespoons grated Parmesan cheese
1 tablespoon chopped parsley
1 pound small shell macaroni
Grated Parmesan cheese, optional

Thaw frozen fish. Cut into 1" chunks. Cook onion until tender but not brown in oil in Dutch oven or 12" frypan. Add fish, 1 teaspoon salt and pepper; cover and cook until fish flakes easily when tested with a fork, about 10 minutes. Add water, tomato paste, shrimp, vegetables, olives (if used), Parmesan cheese, parsley and remaining 1 teaspoon salt. Cover and simmer until shrimp is cooked and vegetables are tender, about 10 minutes. Cook macaroni as directed on package label. Drain well. Combine macaroni and fish mixture and mix carefully; heat thoroughly, about 5 minutes. Sprinkle generously with additional Parmesan cheese before serving, if desired.

POLLOCK THERMIDOR
Serves 8 - 10

2½ pounds pollock fillets
1 stick butter
¼ cup parsley, chopped
1 quart milk
2 six-ounce packages yellow
American cheese

1 onion, chopped
½ green pepper, chopped
4 tablespoons flour
dash pepper
1 teaspoon salt

Simmer pollock in small amount of water 10 minutes or until fish flakes easily. Drain and flake. Saute chopped vegetables in ½ stick butter 5 minutes. Melt ½ stick butter. Stir in flour and seasonings. Add milk and cook until thickened, stirring constantly. Add cheese and continue heating until cheese is melted. Add fish and vegetables to sauce and pour in casserole.

Topping
1 stick butter
½ box Ritz crackers, crumbled
½ teaspoon salt

½ cup mayonnaise
½ cup seasoned bread crumbs
dash pepper

Melt butter, add other ingredients and mix well. Cover casserole with topping. Bake uncovered at 350°F. for 15 minutes.

WHITING PIEMONTESE
Serves 6 - 8

1½ pounds whiting fillets
4 cups water, divided
1 cup yellow corn meal
1 teaspoon salt
4 tablespoons butter
¼ pound grated Parmesan cheese
⅛ teaspoon pepper
2 10-ounce packages frozen
  chopped spinach

1 teaspoon oregano
½ teaspoon salt
1 tablespoon lemon juice
Flour
Parsley
½ cup dry white wine
½ cup tomato puree

Bring 3 cups water to boiling. Combine remaining cold water, corn meal and 1 teaspoon salt; stir into boiling water. Cook until thickened, stirring often. Cover; cook over low heat 10 minutes longer. Remove from heat and stir in butter, cheese, and pepper. Stir until butter and cheese are melted. Meanwhile, cook spinach according to package directions; season with oregano, ½ teaspoon salt and lemon juice. Dust whiting fillets with flour. Saute in butter or vegetable oil until golden brown. Spread the corn meal mixture (polenta) on the bottom of an oval serving dish, top with spinach. Arrange fillets on spinach. Sprinkle with chopped parsely. Add wine and tomato puree to pan juices; blend well. Pour over fish.

FISH-NOODLE CASSEROLE
Serves 6 - 8

2 pounds fish fillets
3 tablespoons butter
1 can (3½ ounces) French fried
  onions
4 cups (4 ounces raw weight)
  medium noodles, cooked and
  drained
¼ cup chopped pimientos

1 can (4 ounces) sliced mushrooms
  drained
2 cans (10 3/4 ounce each)
  condensed cheddar cheese soup
1 cup milk
1 teaspoon paprika
1 teaspoon salt
1 teaspoon Worcestershire sauce

Cut fish into 1" pieces. Cook fish in 10" fry pan in butter, turning fish carefully, until firm. Save ½ cup onions for topping. Combine fish, noodles, mushrooms, pimientos, and remaining onions in large mixing bowl. Combine soup, milk and seasonings in saucepan. Heat and stir until smooth. Pour over fish mixture and stir carefully. Pour into baking dish, 12 x 8 x 2 inches. Bake in a moderate oven, 350°F, 30 minutes or until mixture is hot and bubbles around edges. Sprinkle the reserve onions around edge of baking dish 5 minutes before end of baking time.

SPINACH FISH CASSEROLE
Serves 4

1-2 pounds hake fillets
1 package fresh spinach
½ pound grated cheddar cheese
1 medium onion, chopped fine
½ cup finely chopped celery
2 medium potatoes cooked and mashed
1 beaten egg

Saute fish, onion, celery, and salt and pepper to taste in oil for about 10 minutes in a large frypan. Set aside to cool slightly. Cook spinach and drain, then squeeze of all water. Set aside and cool. Add mashed potatoes, fish, onions, celery, salt, pepper and beaten egg together. Butter casserole dish, put layer of fish mixture in casserole then layer of spinach, sprinkle with half of grated cheese. Add the rest of fish mixture on top, then spinach and sprinkle remaining cheese over spinach. Bake in 350°F. for 25-30 minutes until just heated and cheese melts. Serve with a white sauce or fish sauce. (see sauces)

TUNA-SEASHELL CASSEROLE
Serves 4 - 6

½ pound large shell spaghetti
½ cup diced green pepper
2 tablespoons butter
½ teaspoon salt
Melted butter
2 (7 ounce) cans drained tunafish, flaked
1 pint jar marinara sauce
1½ cups chopped cooked broccoli or cooked artichoke hearts

Cook shells according to package directions. Melt butter in a skillet; saute green pepper until soft. Combine with salt, sauce, shells, and tuna. Turn mixture into a 2-quart casserole. Arrange vegetables around edge; brush with melted butter. Bake in a moderately hot oven 375°F., 25 minutes or until bubbly.

MARINER'S STEW
Serves 8

2 pounds haddock fillets or
   perch fillets, diced
2 cups canned tomatoes
1 tablespoon flour
1½ cups sliced onions
2 teaspoons salt
½ teaspoon ground black pepper
3/4 teaspoon crumbled oregano leaves
¼ teaspoon powdered mustard
¼ teaspoon whole allspice
1 small ginger root
2 tablespoons butter
2 large eggs, beaten
2 tablespoons fresh lime or lemon juice
1 tablespoon parsley flakes

Place tomatoes in a 2-quart saucepan and break up with a fork. Add flour and mix until smooth. Add onions, butter, salt, pepper, parsley flakes, oregano leaves and powdered mustard. Tie allspice and ginger in a bag, add and cook, covered, for 15 minutes. Add fish and cook 10 minutes or until fish is flaky. Remove from heat and discard spice bag. Stir in beaten eggs. Add lime or lemon juice. Cook until slightly thickened, 2 to 3 minutes. Serve hot.

FISH SOUFFLE
Serves 6

6 tablespoons butter or margarine
½ cup all purpose flour
2 teaspoons salt
¼ teaspoon pepper
2¼ cups milk

6 eggs separated
3 cups cooked, flaked flounder
1 tablespoon grated onion and juice
1 tablespoon butter or margarine
2 tablespoons bread crumbs

Melt 6 tablespoons butter; blend in flour, salt and pepper. Stir in milk, stir over moderate heat until smooth and thickened. Beat egg yolks; add a little of the hot sauce; beat into remaining sauce. Stir in flaked fish and grated onion. Cool. Beat egg white stiff but not dry; fold into fish mixture. Use remaining 1 tablespoon butter to grease 2-quart souffle dish. Coat evenly with bread crumbs. Spoon fish mixture into souffle dish. Bake at 325°F. until deep golden brown and set, about 1 to 1¼ hours. Serve immediately. If desired, a sauce such as tomato or mushroom may be served with the souffle.

FRIDAY CASSEROLE
Serves 2 - 3

1 can tuna or crab or shrimp
1 cup medium white sauce
  (see sauces)

Grated Parmesan cheese
2 tablespoons flour
1 cup milk

Cooked vegetables (leftovers) such as peas, carrots, string beans, lima beans.

Flake fish in buttered casserole. Add vegetables. Pour cream sauce over all. Make sauce by cooking together butter and flour, and slowly stirring in milk. Cook and stir until sauce is smooth and thickened. Sprinkle cheese over top. Bake at 350°F. until sauce is hot, bubbly and cheese is melted.

COD FILLETS WITH EGG NOODLES
Serves 6

1 package (8 ounces) egg noodles
3 tablespoons butter
3 tablespoons flour
3 cups milk
1 tablespoon lemon juice
1 teaspoon each dry mustard and Worcestershire sauce
½ teaspoon salt

1/8 teaspoon each pepper and nutmeg
1½ cups shredded sharp cheddar cheese, divided
2 packages (10 ounces each) frozen chopped spinach thawed and drained
1½ pounds cod fillets
¼ cup toasted slivered almonds

Cook noodles as directed on package until tender; drain. Meanwhile, melt butter; blend in flour. Add milk; stir over medium heat until smooth and thickened. Stir in lemon juice, mustard, Worcestershire sauce, salt, pepper, nutmeg and 1 cup of the cheese. Combine cooked noodles with half the cheese sauce. Pour into 2 quart baking dish. Top with spinach. Arrange fish fillets on spinach. Pour remaining sauce over fish. Sprinkle with remaining cheese and almonds. Bake at 375°F. for 25 minutes, or until fish is cooked.

FISH FILLETS WITH TOMATO RICE
Serves 4

1 pound fresh fish fillets
  (ocean perch, flounder, sole,
  haddock, cod)
½ cup rice

1 teaspoon oregano
freshly ground pepper
½ teaspoon salt
1 (1 pound) can tomatoes (2 cups)

Place fresh fish fillets in a buttered 1½ quart baking dish. Pour rice around fish; sprinkle with oregano, pepper and salt and pour tomatoes over fish and rice. If tomatoes are whole, break up with a fork. Cover dish with foil and bake in a 375°F. oven about 50 minutes or until fish flakes easily and rice is tender.

FISH SANDWICH LOAF
Serves 6

1 pound fish fillets
1 cup boiling water
1 onion slice
2 tablespoons lemon juice
3/4 teaspoon salt
1 loaf Vienna bread, about 14
  inches long

½ cup salad dressing
½ cup chili sauce
½ cup chopped dill pickles
¼ cup sliced green onions
1 cup shredded cheddar cheese
1 tablespoon horseradish

Place fish in a 10-inch fry pan. Add water, onion slice, lemon juice, and ½ teaspoon salt. Cover and simmer 5 to 10 minutes or until fish flakes easily. Remove fish from liquid; drain and chill. Flake. Cut loaf of bread in half lengthwise. Hollow out top and bottom halves leaving an outside shell 3/4-inch thick. Tear bread removed from center of loaf into small pieces. Combine remaining ingredients, flaked fish and bread pieces; mix well. Pile into bottom shell and mound up. Place top shell over filling. Wrap loaf securely in aluminum foil. Bake in a hot oven 400°F., 40 minutes or until loaf is hot. Cut in thick chunks or slices.

FISH FILLET AND VEGETABLE MEDLEY
Serves 4 - 6

2 packages (1 pound each) frozen fish
  fillets (cod or whiting) completely
  thawed
salt and pepper
paprika

1 package (10 ounce) frozen
  mixed vegetables
2 tablespoons butter or
  margarine
⅓ cup light cream, heated

Cut fish in 6 portions and drain on paper towels. Put skin side down, in buttered shallow baking dish. Sprinkle with salt, pepper and paprika and arrange vegetables around and between fillets. Dot with butter and bake in hot oven (400°F.) 20 minutes. Pour cream on top and bake 5 minutes longer, or until fish is opaque and flakes easily.

BAKED

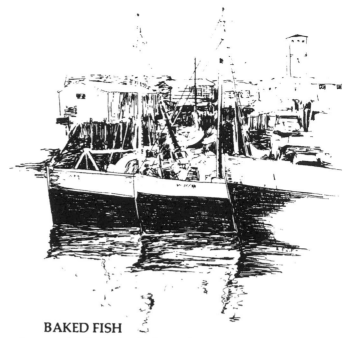

BAKED FISH

Fish weighing 3 to 5 pounds may be baked whole, either with or without stuffing. The head and tail may be removed or left on. Clean fish, dry and rub salt in the inside. Stuff if desired and sew or skewer. Place a sheet of greased heavy or parchment paper in baking pan, making it large enough so that it can be used to lift fish from pan when done. Place a bay leaf and a few slices of onion and bacon or salt pork on the paper and lay the fish on top. If fish is lean, cut a few slashes down its back and place a strip of salt pork in each. Bake in quick or hot oven (425°F.) 10 minutes.

FISH FILLETS IN RED WINE
Serves 4

4 fish fillets
3/4 cup sliced mushrooms
3 tablespoons butter
3 tablespoons sherry
½ teaspoon salt
dash freshly ground pepper
3 tablespoons flour

3/4 cup red wine
3/4 cup consommé
1 teaspoon minced parsley
2 tablespoons finely chopped
  scallions
¼ cup light cream
¼ cup grated American cheese
paprika

Place fish fillets in a greased, 12-inch casserole. Cook mushrooms in butter until tender. Add sherry, salt and pepper and simmer, covered, 3 minutes longer. Remove from heat and blend in flour. Gradually stir in wine and consomme. Cook over low heat, stirring constantly, until mixture comes to a boil. Add parsley, scallions, and cream. Pour over fish and sprinkle with cheese. Bake at 375°F. about 20 minutes. Just before serving, sprinkle with paprika.

BAKED FILLETS WITH STUFFING
Serves 6

4 cups day-old bread, cubed
1/2 cup minced celery
1/2 teaspoon salt
3/4 cup poultry seasoning
6 eight ounce portions Boston
  Bluefish (pollock) fillets or
  other fish fillets, fresh or frozen

1/4 cup minced onion
1/2 cup melted butter or margarine
1/4 teaspoon pepper
1 cup broth or stock
1/4 cup bacon, cooked and crumbled
1/4 cup stuffed olives, chopped

Thaw fish. Saute onion and celery in 1/4 cup hot butter. Mix with bread. Add seasonings and toss to mix. Add broth about 1/4 cup at a time and mix well. Stuffing should not be too soggy. Spread stuffing in thin layers in a greased shallow baking pan. Arrange fillets on top of stuffing. Mix remaining 1/4 cup butter, bacon, and olives. Sprinkle over fillets. Bake in a moderate oven, 350°F. 35 to 40 minutes, or until fish is fork tender. To serve, use a bread spatula to lift fish and stuffing together. Serve with buttered squash and fried onions.

BAKED STRIPED BASS WITH CLAMS
Serves 8

1 dozen hard-shelled clams
1 4 1/4 pound striped bass,
  dressed and boned with tail on
1 teaspoon salt
1/4 teaspoon basil
1/8 teaspoon pepper
1/2 cup parsley sprigs

1 medium onion thinly sliced
2 celery stalks, with leaves, chopped
1 garlic clove, halved
2 bay leaves
1/2 cup dry white wine
1/2 cup butter or margarine, melted

About 50 minutes before serving:
Preheat oven to 350°F. Scrub clams under cold running water; set aside. Sprinkle inside of fish with salt, basil, and pepper. Arrange parsley and half of onion slices inside fish; place fish in large, shallow baking pan or ovenproof serving dish. Around fish, place clams, remaining onion, celery, garlic and bay leaves. Pour wine and butter or margarine over fish. Cover pan with foil and bake 40 to 50 minutes until fish flakes easily when tested with a fork and shells or clams are open. Discard garlic and bay leaves.

BAKED FISH FIESTA
Serves 6

2 pounds cusk, cod or other firm fish fillets, fresh or frozen
¾ cup fine dry bread crumbs
¼ cup grated Parmesan cheese
2 tablespoons chopped parsley
1 teaspoon salt
¼ teaspoon pepper
1 small garlic clove, minced
¼ cup cooking oil
3 slices bacon, diced
1 can (8 ounce) stewed tomatoes
2 hard-boiled eggs, sliced

Thaw frozen fish, cut into 6 equal portions. Combine crumbs, 2 tablespoons cheese, parsley, salt pepper and garlic. Dip fish in oil, drain and dip in crumb mixture. Place fillets in individual baking pan or baking sheet. Fry bacon pieces until half done; drain well. Top each fish portion with an equal amount of bacon, tomato pieces and egg slices. Sprinkle with remaining 2 tablespoons of cheese. Bake in moderate oven, 375° degrees, 20 minutes or until fish flakes easily when tested with a fork.

FISH FLORENTINE
Serves 4 - 6

2 packages frozen spinach
4 tablespoons melted butter or margarine (divided)
2 tablespoons lemon juice
¼ cup minced onion
2 pounds haddock, cod, pollock
cheese sauce (see sauces)

Cook spinach as directed on package. Cook onion in 2 tablespoons butter until tender. Place fish fillets in greased shallow baking dish. Dot with remaining butter. Sprinkle with lemon juice. Cover with spinach and top with cheese sauce. Cook in 350°F., for 15 minutes, or until fish flakes easily.

FILLETS OF COD CAPE ANN STYLE
Serves 2

1 pound cod
2 tablespoons shallots
6 mushrooms, chopped
2 tablespoons white wine
salt and pepper
parsley
2 tablespoons flour
½ cup milk
lemon slices
cucumber balls
tomato wedges

Arrange fillets of cod in buttered baking dish. Sprinkle with chopped mushrooms, parsley, shallots, salt and pepper. Moisten with white wine. Bake at 350°F. for 15 minutes; remove to serving platter. Combine flour and milk with remaining juices. Cook, stirring, until sauce is smooth and slightly thickened. Pour over fish in serving platter. Garnish with lemon slices, cucumber balls, and tomato wedges.

33

BAKED WHITING
Serves 4

6 whiting (about ½ pound each) de-headed	¼ cup milk
1 teaspoon salt	1 teaspoon salt
dash pepper	3/4 cup toasted dry bread crumbs
1 cup chopped parsley	½ cup grated Swiss cheese
¼ cup butter, softened	3 tablespoons melted fat or oil
	1 egg, beaten

Clean, wash, and dry fish; sprinkle inside with salt and pepper. Add parsley to butter and mix thoroughly. Spread inside of each fish with approximately 1 tablespoon parsley butter. Combine egg, milk, and salt. Combine crumbs and cheese. Dip fish in egg mixture and roll in crumb mixture. Place on well-greased cookie sheet, 12 by 15 inches. Sprinkle remaining crumb mixture over top of fish. Bake in an extremely hot oven 500°F., for 10 minutes or until fish flakes easily.

OVEN "FRIED" WHITING
Serves 4

6 to 8 whiting (about ½ pound each, de-headed)	evaporated milk
seasoned salt	1 cup packaged cornflake crumbs
2 tablespoons lemon juice	3 tablespoons butter

Rinse fish in cold water; pat dry with paper towelling. Sprinkle body cavity with salt and lemon juice. Dip fish first in evaporated milk, then in cornflake crumbs. Place in shallow baking pan lined with aluminum foil. Dot with butter. Bake at 425°F., about 20 minutes, or until fish flakes easily. Garnish with lemon.

PRIDE OF GLOUCESTER
Serves 6 - 8
Cut 2 pounds whiting fillets (or other fish fillets) into 3 pieces each.

Mix:

3/4 cup bread crumbs	¼ teaspoon pepper
¼ cup Romano cheese, grated	1 teaspoon salt
1 large clove garlic minced	2 tablespoons parsley, chopped

Beat 2 eggs. Dip fish into eggs. Roll fish in bread crumb mixture. Fry in 3/4 cup hot oil. Set aside. Drain oil that is left from frying fish into a saucepan, add & saute:

2 cups onion and 2 cups green pepper, sliced.

Add: 2 cups stewed tomatoes, salt & pepper to taste

Cook sauce until vegetables are tender. Arrange fish in baking dish, pour sauce over fish. Bake, covered, 350°F., for 30 minutes. If desired cook 1 pound thin spaghetti and arrange fish and sauce over it. Sprinkle with Parmesan cheese.

FLOUNDER PINWHEELS
Serves 6

2 pounds flounder, cusk or
   other firm fish fillets
3/4 cup fine dry bread crumbs
¼ cup grated Parmesan cheese

¼ teaspoon pepper
1 teaspoon salt
½ cup mayonnaise
2 tablespoons chopped parsley

Cut each fillet in two lengthwise strips and brush with mayonnaise. Roll in the bread mixture. Roll up jelly roll style and place upright in buttered dish, 9 x 12. Cover with tinfoil and bake at 375°F. for 30 minutes. Remove cover and bake for 5 more minutes.

FLOUNDER ROLL-UPS
Serves 6 - 8

12 large flounder filletts
8 strips bacon, diced
½ cup melted butter
6 cups cornbread crumbs

½ teaspoon dried chervil
½ teaspoon dried tarragon leaves
hot water
butter

Cook bacon crisp; drain on absorbent paper. Strain bacon drippings; measure ¼ cup and add to melted butter. Combine cornbread crumbs, bacon, herbs, and combined fats; mix will. Add enough hot water to make stuffing as moist as desired. Place spoonful of stuffing on each flounder fillets; roll up firmly. Line baking pan with foil. Grease foil. Place roll-ups in pan; dot generously with butter. Bake at 375°F., for 25 minutes, or until fish flakes easily with fork. Serve with your favorite sauce.

MIDDLE BANKS NUGGETS
Serves 4 - 6

1½ pounds white fillets, cut
   into strips 9 in. long, 2
   in. wide
1¼ cups bread crumbs
2 tablespoons chopped parsley
1 clove garlic, minced
1 teaspoon salt
¼ teaspoon pepper

6 tablespoons stewed tomatoes
¼ teaspoon parmesan
   cheese
¼ cup olive oil
2 hard boiled eggs, cut into
   6 pieces each
12 two inch strips provolone cheese

Combine bread crumbs, parsley, parmesan cheese, salt, pepper, and garlic. Dip fish in oil and roll in bread crumb mixture. Place 1 piece provolone, 1 piece hard boiled egg and 1 tablespoon stewed tomato on fish. Roll jelly roll style and place upright in greased dish. Spoon remaining tomato over top, sprinkle with rest of crumbs and oil. Bake covered at 375°F. for 30 minutes and uncovered for 5 minutes more.

FISHERMAN'S CABBAGE ROLLS OR GREEN PEPPER RINGS
Serves 6

1 pound pollock
1 cup cooked rice
½ stick butter
1 med. onion, chopped
1 stalk celery, chopped
2 hard boiled eggs, cut into
   small pieces

2 raw eggs
3 tablespoons butter
½ cup plus 3 tablespoons, grated
   Romano cheese
salt and pepper to taste
1 small can stewed tomatoes
1 med. cabbage or 3 green peppers

Filling

Saute onions and celery in butter for 10 minutes. Add fish, salt and pepper. Cover and simmer until fish flakes easily. Add rice, hard boiled eggs, ½ cup cheese and 2 raw eggs. Mix well.

Cabbage Rolls

Remove large leaves from cabbage. Trim off thick part of each leaf. Cover leaves with boiling water and let stand until they become limp. Place a mound of filling on each cabbage leaf. Loosely fold over sides of leaf and roll up. Place, with seam side down, on well greased baking dish. Pour tomatoes over rolls and sprinkle with 3 tablespoons grated cheese. Cover with tinfoil and bake at 375°F., for 20 minutes. Will make 15-20 rolls. Remove foil last 2 minutes of baking.

Green Pepper Rings

Cut green pepper into ½ inch rings and place in well greased baking dish. Add filling to rings, cover with tomatoes and sprinkle with 3 tablespoons grated cheese. Cover with tinfoil and bake at 375°F., for 20 minutes. Peppers may be cut lengthwise, cleaned and filled.

FISH PARMIGIANA
Serves 6

6 frozen breaded fish portions
   (4 ounces each)
⅓ cup cooking oil
½ cup thinly sliced onion
1 jar (15 to 15½ ounces)
   meatless spaghetti sauce

6 slices (3 x4½ or 5-inches
   each) mozzarella cheese
   (about 3 ounces)
2 tablespoons grated
   Parmesan cheese

Arrange fish portions on greased shallow baking pan. Drizzle 3 tablespoons of oil over portions. Bake in very hot oven, 500°F., until lightly browned, 15 to 20 minutes. Cook onion until tender in remaining oil. Add spaghetti sauce; heat. Pour ½ of the sauce over bottom of shallow 2-quart casserole. Arrange fish portions in a row down center of casserole overlapping portions slightly. Pour remaining sauce over fish. Top with mozzarella cheese slices and sprinkle Parmesan cheese over top. Return to oven until cheese melts, 5 to 8 minutes.

FILLET OF SOLE MARGUERY
Serves 4

8 jumbo shrimp
12 clams, scrubbed clean
5 tablespoons dry white wine
1 cup clam broth
¼ teaspoon salt
¼ teaspoon thyme
1 bay leaf

juice of ½ lemon
3 tablespoons butter
2 egg yolks, slightly beaten
1 tablespoon heavy cream
1½ pounds fillet of sole
1½ tablespoons flour

Boil shrimp 3 minutes, shell and devein. Place clams in covered saucepan with one tablespoon wine and cook until clamshells open. Remove clams from shells. Strain juice, mix with 1 extra cup clam broth, add 2 tablespoons wine, salt, thyme, bay leaf, lemon juice and boil gently 20 minutes. Strain and save liquid. Place sole in well-buttered baking dish, add just enough clam liquid to cover bottom of dish. Add 2 tablespoons wine. Dot with butter. Cover and bake 375°F., for 12 minutes. Remove from oven, add shrimp and clams, and keep warm.

Blend together 2 tablespoons butter and flour, add remaining clam liquid and gravy from baking dish. Mix well. Add egg yolks and cream, mix with beater until smooth. Place over very low heat and cook until slightly thick. Add butter a little at a time, mixing constantly. Pour sauce over fish in baking dish. Bake at 400°F., for 3 minutes.

ELEGANT AND EASY AuGRATIN
Serves 4 - 6

1½ pounds sole or flounder fillets
½ lemon
salt and pepper
1 can (10½ ounces) condensed
   cream of mushroom soup
chopped parsley

1 tablespoon cream sherry (optional)
6 servings seasoned instant mashed
   potato
1 tablespoon fine dry bread crumbs
1 tablespoon grated Parmesan cheese

Rinse fish fillets quickly under running cold water. Drain on paper towels and arrange fillets, slightly over-lapping, in buttered shallow baking dish (not glass). Squeeze lemon juice on top (direct from lemon, removing seeds, if any) and sprinkle lightly with salt and pepper. Cover tightly with foil and bake in a moderate over 350°F., 20 minutes, or until fish flakes easily with fork. Carefully drain off all liquid, holding fish with spatula. Mix fish liquid with soup and sherry until smooth. Pour over fish, and spoon or flute mashed potato around edge. Sprinkle entire surface with mixture of bread crumbs and cheese. (at this point dish may be cooled and refrigerated until 3/4 hour before broiling.) Broil 7 inches from heat 10 minutes, or until top is well browned and dish is bubbling hot. Sprinkle with parsley. Note: Frozen fish fillets, completely thawed and separated, can be used.

FANCY FISH ROLLS
Serves 4

4 large (or 8 small) fish fillets
6 sprigs parsley
2 pimientos
1 large onion
½ cup butter
1 shredded carrot

1 teaspoon celery salt
1 cup bread crumbs
¼ cup grated Italian cheese
1 egg
½ cup water

Mince together the parsley, pimientos, and onions. Cook 3 minutes in butter. Add carrot, celery salt, bread crumbs, cheese, egg, and water. Mix well. Spread on fish fillets, roll up; secure with toothpicks. Brush with butter. Bake at 350°F., for 20 to 30 minutes, depending on size of fish fillets.

SAVORY BAKED HADDOCK
Serves 6

1½ pounds fillet of haddock
salt to taste
½ teaspoon powdered mustard
½ cup mayonnaise
2 teaspoons water

1 teaspoon instant minced onion
½ teaspoon thyme leaves
1 teaspoon fresh lemon juice
dash fresh ground black pepper
paprika

Wipe fish with a damp cloth and arrange in a buttered baking dish. Sprinkle with salt. Soak mustard in water 10 minutes and add to mayonnaise along with onion, lemon juice, thyme leaves, and pepper. Spread on fish. Bake in a preheated moderate over 350°F., 25 minutes or until to is brown and fish is flaky. Garnish with paprika.

BAKED HADDOCK WITH HERBS
Serves 4

2 pounds haddock fillets
3/4 teaspoon salt
¼ teaspoon pepper
sprinkling of garlic powder
sprinkling of tarragon, powdered

⅓ cup sherry
1 cup cream of mushroom soup
½ cup buttered bread crumbs
½ cup grated cheddar cheese

Cut haddock into serving pieces and place in a buttered casserole. Sprinkle on seasoning, add sherry and soup. Top with buttered crumbs blended with grated cheese. Bake in 350°F., for about 30 minutes.

TOMATO CROWN FISH
Serves 4

1½ pounds fish fillet (suggest sliced haddock)
½ green pepper, minced
1½ cups water
2 tablespoons onion, minced
2 tablespoons lemon juice
½ cup bread crumbs
2 large fresh or canned whole tomatoes
1 tablespoon oil
½ teaspoon basil

Freshen 1½ pounds of fish fillets, for several minutes in a mixture of 1½ cups of water and 2 tablespoons of lemon juice. Then place the fish fillet in a greased baking dish and season lightly. Slice 2 large fresh or canned whole tomatoes and place on the fish. Then sprinkle with ½ green pepper, 2 tablespoons of minced onion. Mix ½ cup bread crumbs, 1 tablespoon oil, and ½ teaspoon basil. Sprinkle crumb mixture evenly over the tomatoes. Bake 10-15 minutes in a 350°F., oven.

HALIBUT STEAK WITH TOMATO-BREAD STUFFING
Serves 6

2 pounds halibut fish steaks, 3/4 pound each
3 tablespoons butter, melted
1 teaspoon salt
½ cup canned tomatoes or 2/3 cup chopped fresh tomatoes
1¼ teaspoons ground black pepper
1 teaspoon poultry seasoning
2 cups soft bread crumbs
⅓ cup boiling water
1 tablespoon onion flakes
Lemon-mayonnaise sauce (see sauces)
1 tablespoon parsley flakes

Place one steak in an oiled baking dish. Mix ½ teaspoon of the salt and ¼ teaspoon of the black pepper and sprinkle over fish slices. Combine the remaining salt and pepper with bread crumbs, onion flakes, parsley flakes, butter, tomatoes, and poultry seasoning and spread over fish in sandwich fashion. Cover with second steak. Dot top with the 1½ tablespoons butter. Pour boiling water in pan around fish. Bake in 350°F., oven for 35 minutes or until fish is flaky. Garnish with lemon slices and paprika. Serve with Lemon-Mayonnaise sauce.

BAKED HALIBUT
Serves 6

6 steak pieces halibut or swordfish (medium size)
½ teaspoon pepper
¼ teaspoon garlic salt
2 cups cracker crumbs
½ cup oil for baking
½ cup grated American cheese
½ teaspoon salt

Wash fish thoroughly and drain well. Mix crumbs with cheese; salt and pepper; garlic salt. Oil baking dish. Dip fish into mix and place in dish. Pour ½ cup oil over fish and bake in oven at 350°F., for 25 minutes. Serve with lemon wedges.

FILLET OF SOLE THERMIDOR
Serves 6 - 8

2 pounds (about 8) fresh sole fillets
2 tablespoons melted butter
2 teaspoons salt
½ teaspoon seasoned salt
1/8 teaspoon pepper
½ cup milk
Cheese sauce with sherry (see sauces)

About 45 minutes before serving:
Preheat oven to 350°F., In small saucepan, melt butter; use to brush both sides of fillets. Sprinkle salt, seasoned salt and pepper over fillets. Roll up each fillet and place, seam-side down, in 9" by 9" baking dish. Pour ½ cup milk over fillets and bake 25 minutes or until fish flakes easily. When fish is done, remove from oven and preheat broiler. Pour off pan liquid, reserving ¼ cup to stir into cheese sauce. (if not using sherry, use 3 tablespoons more pan liquid.) Pour sauce over fish; sprinkle with paprika. Broil about 1 minute until sauce is slightly golden. If using frozen sole fillets, thaw and separate. Arrange in bottom of 12" by 8 baking pan (do not roll) ; proceed as above.

OVEN-FRIED FISH FILLETS
Serves 6

2 pounds cod, haddock or
   pollock fillets
2 tablespoons lemon juice
¼ cup flour
3/4 teaspoon salt
1 cup finely crushed cornflakes
Tarter sauce
capers, drained
dill or parsley sprigs
½ cup butter or margarine, melted

Rinse fish quickly under running cold water. Drain on paper towels and slice in 6 portions, cutting tail portion slightly larger; fold end of tail under for even cooking. Combine next 4 ingredients, stirring until smooth, in shallow dish or 8 inch piepan. Put cornflakes in another shallow dish. Use a fork and dip fish in flour-butter mixture, then coat fish with cereal. Arrange in single layer in foil-lined baking pan. Bake in hot oven (400°) 20 minutes, or until fish is well browned and flakes easily with fork. Garnish each portion with tarter sauce, a few capers and fresh dill or parsley and serve with additional tarter sauce and boiled or baked potato.

FRIED

THE WHALE'S BITE
2 recipes in one
Serves 8

1½ pounds hake fillets
1 cup chopped celery
1 cup diced potatoes
½ cup chopped onions
1 cup canned tomatoes
1 teaspoon oregano
2 cups water
3/4 cup breadcrumbs
2 tablespoons chopped parsley
3 tablespoons grated Parmesan cheese
salt and pepper to taste

½ teaspoons allspice
2 eggs, beaten
8 fish sticks, cooked
8 strips provolone, ½ inch wide
1 medium onion, sliced
3/4 cup tomato puree
1 tablespoon oil
2 cups of oil for deep frying

Saute sliced onion in oil. Add tomato and oregano. Cook 10 minutes. In a saucepan, simmer potatoes, onion and celery 7-10 minutes in 2 cups water until the potatoes are almost cooked. Add fish fillets, salt and pepper. Cook 10 minutes, stirring occasionally. Drain, leaving some moisture. Mash, adding breadcrumbs, Parmesan, parsley and allspice. Add eggs and mix thoroughly. Spoon ½ cup fish mixture onto waxed paper and spread into a circle 6 inches in diameter. In the center of the circle, place one fish stick, a strip of provolone and 1 tablespoon sauce. Roll circle into sausage.

In a deep pan, heat 2 cups of oil over medium flame. Cook sausages in oil, turning occasionally until golden brown. Remove carefully, being careful not to pierce. Blot with towel to remove excess oil.

Another variation: For a quick meal form fish mixture into patties and deep fry. Blot on paper towels. Try fennel instead of allspice for a flavor variation.

DIFFERENT FRIED FISH
Serves 6

2 pounds dressed fish
(whole fillets or steaks)
1 egg
2 tablespoons water

1 cup prepared biscuit mix
3 tablespoons ketchup
½ cup shortening or oil

Dip fish first in egg beaten with water, then in biscuit mix blended with ketchup. Fry slowly in heated shortening until golden brown on both sides. Serve with lemon and parsley.

SWEET-SOUR FISH
Serves 4 - 6

2 pounds fish fillets
2 tablespoons cornstarch
2 tablespoons peanut oil
1 scallion or ½ medium-sized onion
3 cloves garlic, crushed
1 slice ginger, cut in strips

Mix for Sauce:
3 tablespoons soy sauce
2 tablespoons sherry
1 cup brown sugar
4 tablespoons vinegar
1 teaspoon salt
2 tablespoons cornstarch
1 cup chicken stock or water

Cut fillets into 2-inch by 3-inch pieces. Coat with cornstarch. Heat pan (350°). Add oil, heat thoroughly. Fry fish on both sides until golden brown. Remove from pan. Quick fry scallion, garlic, and ginger until golden brown. Add sweet-sour sauce and bring to a boil. Stir constantly until thick. Reduce the heat to low. Add the fish gently into the sauce. Simmer for 1 minute. Serve hot.

PAN FRIED SMELTS

2 pounds smelts, dressed
½ cup all-purpose flour
1 teaspoon salt
¼ teaspoon pepper
2 eggs

½ cup salad oil
2 tablespoons butter
lime wedges for garnish
½ cup dried bread crumbs

About 1½ hours before serving: On waxed paper, combine flour, salt and pepper. In pie plate, with fork, beat eggs with 2 tablespoons water. Onto second sheet of waxed paper, pour bread crumbs. On another sheet of waxed paper, place a rack. Using tongs, coat fish one by one, in flour, then in egg, then in bread crumbs, and place on rack. Let dry 30 minutes. In large skillet over medium-high heat, in hot oil and butter of margarine, fry fish a few at a time, about 2 minutes on each side until fish flakes easily when tested with a fork. Serve on warm platter, garnish with lime wedges.

FRIED FILLETS OF COD OR POLLOCK
Serves 6

2 pounds cod or pollock
1 egg, slightly beaten
1 cup dry bread crumbs

1 teaspoon salt
1 tablespoon milk
fat or cooking oil

Wash and dry fish. Cut into serving pieces. Sprinkle salt, combine egg and milk. Dip fish in egg mixture then in crumbs. Fry until brown, 5 minutes on each side.

FISH FRITTERS
Serves 4

1 pound fish fillets
3 eggs separated
3 tablespoons flour

1 clove minced garlic
2 tablespoons minced parsley
salt and pepper

Cook fish and mash it. Beat yolks of eggs until light and thick. Then add, little by little, the flour, salt and pepper, the minced garlic and parsley and the fish. Lastly add the whites of the eggs beaten to a froth. Drop spoonfuls of mixture into hot fat 360° and fry to golden brown.

FISH FRY
Serves 6

2 pounds fish fillets
¼ cup evaporated milk
1½ teaspoons salt
dash pepper

½ cup flour
¼ cup yellow cornmeal
1 teaspoon paprika
melted fat or oil

Combine milk, salt and pepper. Combine flour, cornmeal, and paprika. Dip fish in milk mixture and roll in flour mixture. Place fat in a heavy frying pan, and heat until fat is hot but not smoking. Add fish and fry for 4 minutes. Turn carefully and fry for 3 to 4 minutes longer or until fish is brown and flakes easily when tested with a fork. Drain on absorbent paper.

FISH WITH MANDARIN SAUCE
Serves 4 - 6

2 pounds white fish fillets
2 tablespoons cornstarch
1 can bamboo shoots (optional)
6 mushrooms, sliced
1 cup chicken stock
4 tablespoons peanut oil for frying
1 scallion or ½ medium sized
   onion sliced
2 cloves garlic crushed
1 slice ginger, sliced

Mix for Sauce:
½ cup soy sauce
2 tablespoon sherry
1 tablespoon brown sugar
1 teaspoon salt

Cut fillets in 2 inch by 3 inch pieces, coat with cornstarch. Heat pan (325°F.). Add peanut oil, heat thoroughly. Fry fish on both sides until golden brown. Remove from the pan. Quick fry scallion, garlic, and ginger until golden brown, stirring constantly. Add mushrooms and bamboo shoots, and quick fry for 1 minute. Add sauce and chicken stock. Bring to a boil. Add fish. Lower heat. Simmer for 15 minutes covered.

FISH AND CHIPS
Serves 6

2 pounds pollock
(other fish can be used)
1½ cups prepared pancake mix
1½ cups milk
3/4 teaspoon salt

Hot oil for frying
6 servings french fries
malt vinegar or
tartar sauce

Cut fillets in pieces 4 x 1 ½ x ½ inches. Combine pancake mix, milk, and salt, beat until smooth. Dip fish pieces into batter, and place in single layer in fry basket. Fry in deep fat 350°, for 3 to 4 minutes or until coating on fish is brown and fish flakes easily when tested with a fork. Drain on absorbent paper. Serve with hot French fries. Sprinkle fish with malt vinegar or serve with tartar sauce.

ONION-SMOTHERED WHITE FISH
Serves 6

2 pounds any white fish fillets
¼ cup flour
½ teaspoon paprika
½ cup melted fat or oil

1¼ teaspoons salt
4 cups thinly sliced onions
1 cup cider vinegar

Cut fillets into 6 portions. Combine flour and paprika and mix. Sprinkle fish with 1 teaspoon salt. Roll fish in flour mixture. Heat ¼ cup fat in 10-inch fry pan; arrange fish in pan in single layer. Fry over moderate heat 4 to 5 minutes or until brown. Turn carefully. Fry 4 to 5 minutes longer or until fish pieces are lightly browned. While fish is frying cook onions in a second 10-inch fry pan in remaining ¼ cup fat until onions are limp. Add vinegar and remaining ¼ teaspoon salt; simmer uncovered for 10 minutes or until most of the liquid is evaporated. Spoon onion mixture over fish. Cover and cook over low heat for 10 minutes or until the fish flakes easily.

CODFISH BALLS
Serves 4 - 6

1 pound codfish fillets
1 cup breadcrumbs
¼ cup parsley
2 tablespoons Parmesan cheese
2 cloves garlic, minced (or ½ teaspoon garlic powder)

salt
pepper
2 eggs
2 medium-sized potatoes

Boil and mash potatoes, set aside. Boil codfish until it flakes easily. Drain and flake fish with fork. Mix flaked fish and the rest of the ingredients well by hand. Form into cakes, or balls, and fry in hot oil.

MEDITERRANEAN COD OR HADDOCK
Serves 4

2 pounds cod or haddock	salt
2 cups canned tomatoes	pepper
pinch garlic powder	oil or shortening
pinch thyme	parsley, chopped
1 small bay leaf	flour

Make sauce as follows: saute tomatoes, flavor with garlic powder, salt, pepper, bay leaf and thyme. Moisten with white wine to desired consistency; add chopped parsley. Then flour pieces of cod or haddock lightly. Fry briskly in oil or shortening. When golden brown, place fish in baking dish. Pour sauce over the fish before serving.

CODFISH OMELET
Serves 4

1 tablespoon butter	6 eggs, well beaten
2 onions chopped	salt
*1 cup cooked salt fish, shredded	pepper

Fry onions in butter until soft and lightly browned. Add codfish and allow to simmer for a minute or two. Add eggs and stir constantly with a fork until they are just set. Season to taste. *Soak overnight before cooking.

HAKE FISH CAKES
Serves 4

1 pound hake, cut up fine	1 small onion cut up
2 cups bread crumbs	1 tablespoon grated cheese
1 teaspoon salt	2 large eggs
1 teaspoon pepper	1 teaspoon dry parsley

Mix all together and roll into balls, fry in olive oil until brown: Put aside for preparation of sauce.

Sauce for Hake Fish Cakes

1 can tomatoes	½ teaspoon pepper
½ teaspoon salt	1 onion chopped

Cook for 20 minutes then add fish cakes and cook 15 minutes more. (Potatoes may be added if desired).

HALIBUT HOLLANDAISE
Serves 6

2 pounds halibut steaks
2 cups boiling water
1¼ teaspoons salt
1 small onion, sliced
1 small bay leaf
¼ cup butter
2 tablespoons flour

½ cup milk
½ cup water
2 egg yolks, beaten
dash cayenne
2 teaspoons lemon juice
½ teaspoon grated lemon rind
2 tablespoons capers, drained

Cut fish into 6 portions. Place fish in a 10-inch fry pan. Add boiling water, 1 teaspoon salt, onion and bayleaf. Cover and simmer 5 to 10 minutes or until fish flakes easily. Carefully remove fish from liquid; drain. Place fish on a heated serving platter. Keep warm. Melt butter in saucepan; blend in flour, cayenne, and remaining ¼ teaspoon salt. Add milk and water; cook, stirring constantly until smooth and thickened. Add a small amount of hot mixture to egg yolks, beating constantly. Return to hot mixture, and cook about 1 minute. Add lemon juice, rind, and capers; stir. Serve over fish.

HALIBUT STEAK WITH EGGPLANT AND TOMATO SAUCE
Serves 6

1-2 pounds halibut steak
1 large green pepper
1 large onion
1 1 pound eggplant
⅓ cup salad oil
½ cup dry white wine

1 garlic clove, minced
1 bay leaf
¼ cup butter or margarine
2 tablespoons lemon juice
2 8-ounce cans tomato sauce
salt and pepper

About 30 minutes before serving: Cut green pepper into ½ inch strips for sauce: Peel and slice onion. Peel eggplant and cut in ½ inch cubes. In large skillet over medium-high heat, in hot salad oil, cook green pepper and onion until tender; add eggplant, tomato sauce, wine, garlic and bay leaf; simmer 15 minutes. Meanwhile preheat broiler. In small saucepan over low heat, melt butter or margarine with lemon juice, ½ teaspoon salt and ¼ teaspoon pepper, place fish in broiling pan and brush generously with butter mixture. Broil 5 minutes; turn and brush with butter mixture. Broil 5 minutes longer or until fish flakes easily when tested with a fork. Serve with fish sauce.

CAPERED FILLETS OF HADDOCK
Serves 4

4 fillets of haddock or other white fish   flour
3 ounces unsalted butter   salt
1 tablespoon parsley, finely chopped   black pepper
1 tablespoon capers, coarsely chopped

Flour the fish lightly. Put 1 ounce of the butter in a frying pan over a medium heat. When it is foaming, put in the fish. Cook for 5 minutes without touching them. Salt and pepper them. After turning them put the rest of the butter in a small pan, together with the capers, over a low flame. The butter must melt without frying the capers. Put the fish on a serving dish; pour the melted butter and capers over them, and sprinkle with parsley. Serve with plain boiled potatoes.

FRIED MACKEREL WITH RAW SAUCE
Serves 4

2 pounds mackerel fillets   pinch of garlic powder
fine corn meal for coating fish   ¼ teaspoon salt
3/4 cup vinegar   ¼ teaspoon pepper
1 cup water   sprig parsley, cut fine
½ onion, cut fine

Salt mackerel about 1 hour before frying. Then wash and dry the fish. Dip in corn meal. Fry in deep fat and dip in sauce while hot. To make raw sauce mix all ingredients, except the fish and corn meal.

MACKEREL ON THE RUN
Serves 6

2½ - 3 pounds mackerel   3/4 cup flour
2 large onions, sliced   salt and pepper to taste
1 cup vinegar   1 cup cooking oil

Split mackerel lengthwise and cut into portions desired. Sprinkle with salt and roll in flour, fry in hot oil. When evenly browned, drain on paper towel and place on serving platter. Drain oil from pan reserving 3 tablespoons. In same pan, add the oil, sliced onions, saute, salt and pepper to taste, when tender, add vinegar and bring to boil. Pour onion mixture over fish. If fish absorbs vinegar, add ¼ cup more if desired. Chill.
Recommended for picnics.
Note: Any fish rich in fats lends itself to this dish, e.g., halibut.

POLLOCK CAKES
Serves 4 - 6

1 pound pollock fillets
1 cup bread crumbs
2 large cloves garlic
  (chopped fine)
1 teaspoon salt
cooking oil

1½ cups potatoes, diced
¼ cup grated cheese (Parmesan)
1 teaspoon parsley flakes
dash pepper
2 eggs

Cover potatoes with water and bring to a boil. Add fish and continue boiling until potatoes are tender and fish flakes easily. Drain and cool 10 minutes. Mash. Add crumbs, cheese, garlic, parsley flakes, salt, pepper and eggs. Mix well. Shape into cakes and fry in cooking oil at 375° until brown, Drain on absorbent paper.

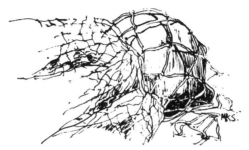

POLLOCK CUTLETS
Serves 4 - 6

1 pound pollock fillets
  (cut into 2-inch squares)
½ cup flour
cooking oil
salt

Bread crumb mixture:
  1 cup fine bread crumbs
  1 small clove garlic, finely
    chopped
  ½ teaspoon salt
  2 tablespoons grated Parmesan
    cheese
½ teaspoon parsley flakes
dash pepper

Combine bread crumb mixture and set aside.

Batter:

2 eggs
dash parsley flakes

1 teaspoon grated cheese
dash pepper

Beat eggs and add cheese, parsley and pepper.

Lightly salt fish squares. Roll squares in flour, dip in batter and roll in bread crumbs mixture. Fry in oil, 375° until brown. Drain on absorbent paper.

BOAT VINCIE N. OCEAN PERCH ROYAL
Serves 8 - 10

1 pound ocean perch
6 cups water
1 cup sliced celery
1 cup diced fresh tomato (1 small)
½ cup chopped onion
3 tablespoons olive oil
1 teaspoon whole allspice
   (tied in cloth)
2¼ teaspoons salt
⅓ cup instant mashed potatoes

2 tablespoons grated
   parmesan cheese
1 tablespoon chopped parsley
dash pepper
2 eggs
10 large escarole leaves
   (5 cups-cut in pieces)
1 can chick peas (15½ ounces
   garbanzos) drained
grated Parmesan cheese
   optional

Cut fish into 1½ inch chunks. Combine water, celery, tomato, onion, oil, allspice and 2 teaspoons salt in Dutch Oven. Simmer 10 minutes. Add fish; cook until fish flakes easily when tested with a fork, 5 to 8 minutes. Remove fish from broth and skin. Combine fish with instant mashed potatoes, cheese, parsley, ¼ teaspoon salt, pepper and eggs; mix well until mixture holds together. Shape into balls, using 1 tablespoon for each. Bring broth to boil. Add escarole and chick peas; bring to boil again. Add fish balls; cook until fish balls are done, 12 to 15 minutes. Remove allspice. Serve with additional Parmesan cheese, if desired.

FISH COOKED IN SOUR CREAM
Serves 4

1½ pounds of haddock, halibut,
   or flounder
¼ cup minced onion
2 tablespoons butter
1½ cups sour cream
½ teaspoon salt

½ teaspoon paprika
2 egg yolks, beaten
salt
1½ teaspoons lemon juice
½ teaspoon dried basil

Clean and cut fish into small pieces. Saute the onion in the butter until golden, but not brown. Stir in and bring to boiling point, but do not boil, the sour cream, salt and paprika. Add the fish gently and gradually. Simmer for 5 minutes and then remove fish to a hot platter. Pour some of the cream over the well-beaten egg yolks and return to rest of cream. Over low heat cook the sauce, stirring constantly, until eggs thicken slightly. Add seasonings. Pour sauce over fish and serve hot.

BROILED AND GRILLED

BROILED FISH

To broil a whole fish, continue the slit made in cleaning the fish so that it can be opened flat. Dry and season with salt, pepper and lemon juice. Place skin side up on greased shallow pan and brown skin quickly under broiler. Turn carefully and cook flesh side 6 to 12 minutes, depending on thickness. Fillets are cooked 4 to 6 minutes on each side. Do not overcook. Fat fish needs no basting but lean fish should be basted well with butter during broiling.

LEMON-BUTTER SALMON STEAKS
Serves 6

2 pounds salmon steaks,
  or other fish steaks (fresh or frozen)
½ cup butter or margarine, melted
2 tablespoons lemon juice

1 tablespoon chopped parsley
1 tablespoon liquid smoke
2 teaspoons salt
dash of pepper

Thaw frozen steaks. Cut into serving-size portions. Combine remaining ingredients. Baste fish with sauce. Place fish in well-greased hinged wire grills. Cook about 4 inches from moderately hot coals for 8 minutes. Baste with sauce. Turn and cook for 7 to 10 minutes longer or until fish flakes easily when tested with a fork.

ITALIAN STYLE HALIBUT STEAKS
Serves 6

2 pounds halibut steaks, or other
  fish steaks, fresh or frozen
2 cups Italian dressing
paprika to taste

2 tablespoons lemon juice
2 teaspoons salt
¼ teaspoon pepper

Thaw frozen steaks. Cut into serving-size portions and place in single layer in a shallow baking dish. Combine remaining ingredients except paprika. Pour sauce over fish and let stand for 30 minutes, turning once. Remove fish, reserving sauce for basting. Place fish in well-greased hinged wire grills. Sprinkle with paprika. Turn and cook for 7 to 10 minutes longer or until fish flakes easily when tested with a fork.

WHITE FISH FILLETS AMANDINE
Serves 6

2 pounds pollock (or other fish fillets)
¼ cup flour
¼ cup melted butter
½ cup sliced almonds
2 tablespoons lemon juice

1 teaspoon seasoned salt
1 teaspoon paprika
4 to 5 drops liquid hot pepper sauce
1 tablespoon chopped parsely

Cut fillets into 6 portions. Combine flour, seasoned salt, and paprika; mix well. Roll fish in flour mixture. Place fish in a single layer, skin side down, in a well-greased baking pan, 15 x 10 x 1 inches. Drizzle 2 tablespoons melted butter over fish. Broil about 4 inches from source of heat 10 to 15 minutes or until fish flakes easily when tested with a fork. While fish is broiling, saute almonds in remaining butter in fry pan and allow to turn a golden brown, stirring constantly. Remove from heat. Add lemon juice, hot pepper sauce, and parsely; mix. Pour over fish. Serve at once.

BROILED POLLOCK STEAKS

Have the steaks cut 1 to 1¼ inches thick, allowing ½ pound for each person. Brush generously with soft butter or margarine. Place in a flat pan lined with aluminum foil. Place in broiler with surface of fish about 3 inches below heat. Broil 5 minutes; turn carefully. Broil 6 to 7 minutes longer or until golden brown or until fish flakes easily with a fork. Remove from broiler. Season to taste with salt and pepper. Serve with Festival Sauce. (See sauces).

BARBEQUED POLLOCK
Serves 6

Pollock fillets, or other fish
  fillets, fresh or frozen (2 pounds)
¼ cup melted fat
¼ cup brown sugar
1 tablespoon mustard
kidney beans and rice, cooked

1 cup chopped onions
1 can tomatoes (1 pound 12 ounces)
3 tablespoons vinegar
1 teaspoon salt

If the fillets are frozen, let them thaw. Cut fish into pieces about an inch square. Fry onion in fat until well cooked. Add everything except beans and rice. Cover and cook slowly for 15 minutes or until fish flakes easily. Serve the barbeque over cooked beans and rice.

51

MEDITERRANEAN BROILED FISH
Serves 6

2 pounds fillet of haddock
½ inch thick
⅓ cup fresh lemon juice
1 teaspoon mint flakes
2 teaspoons oregano leaves

1¼ teaspoons salt
¼ teaspoon ground black pepper
2 tablespoons butter, or olive oil
parsely or lemon slices

Wipe fish with a damp cloth. Place serving-size pieces on a broiler rack. Combine lemon juice, mint flakes, oregano leaves, salt, and pepper and brush over fish. then brush with melted butter, or olive oil. Place under preheated broiler 4 inches from the source of heat. Broil for 5 minutes. Turn fish; brush with seasoned lemon juice and butter, or oil. Broil 5 minutes or until brown. Brush again with seasoned lemon juice; serve hot. Garnish with parsley or thin lemon slices.

ZESTY MULLET FILLETS
Serves 6

2 pounds mullet fillets or other fish
fillets, fresh or frozen
1 tablespoon lemon juice

¼ cup French Dressing
1 tablespoon grated onion
2 teaspoons salt
dash pepper

Thaw frozen fillets. Cut into serving-size portions. Combine remaining ingredients. Baste fish with sauce. Place in well-greased, hinged wire grills. Cook about 4 inches from moderately hot coals for 8 minutes. Baste with sauce. Turn and cook for 7 to 10 minutes longer or until fish flakes easily when tested with a fork.

FISH-KABOBS
Serves 8

4 cloves garlic
1 teaspoon crushed red peppers
1 teaspoon paprika
1 tablespoon salt

1 cup wine vinegar
2 cups water
2 bay leaves crushed
4 to 5 pounds haddock fillets

Combine all ingredients except the last. Pour over haddock fillets, marinate overnight. Drain fish; save marinade. Cut fillets in long strips about 1 inch wide; wind on skewers, making loops in opposite directions, running skewer through fish at each turn. Place on grill about 4 inches above coals. Broil about 15 minutes, or until fish flakes easily, and is golden brown, turning often and brushing with marinade. Serve in Portuguese buns, if available, or in frankfurter rolls which have been heated on the grill.

BARBECUED HADDOCK FILLETS
Serves 6

2 pounds haddock fillets or other
    fish fillets, fresh or frozen
¼ cup chopped onion
2 tablespoons chopped green pepper
1 tablespoon sugar
1 clove garlic, finely chopped
2 tablespoons melted fat or oil

1 can (8 ounces) tomato sauce
2 tablespoons lemon juice
1 tablespoon Worcestershire sauce
2 teaspoons salt
¼ teaspoon pepper

Thaw frozen fillets. Cook onion, green pepper, and garlic in fat until tender. Add remaining ingredients and simmer for 5 minutes, stirring occasionally. Cool. Cut fillets into serving size portions and place in a single layer in a shallow baking dish. Pour sauce over fish and let stand for 30 minutes, turning once. Remove fish, reserving sauce for basting. Place fish in well-greased, hinged wire grills. Cook about 4 inches from moderately hot coals for 8 minutes. Baste with sauce. Turn and cook for 7 to 10 minutes longer or until fish flakes easily when tested with a fork.

SWORDFISH CAPER
Serves 6

2 pounds swordfish steaks, or other
    fish steaks, fresh or frozen
½ cup melted fat or oil
⅓ cup lemon juice
¼ cup chopped onion
2 tablespoons capers and juice
2 tablespoons catsup

¼ teaspoon salt
2 teaspoons Worcestershire sauce
2 teaspoons sugar
4 bay leaves, crushed
2 cloves garlic, finely chopped
paprika

Thaw frozen steaks. Cut into serving-size portions and place in a single layer in a shallow baking dish. Combine remaining ingredients, except paprika. Pour sauce over fish and let stand for 30 minutes, turning once. Remove fish, reserving sauce for basting. Place fish in well-greased, hinged wire grills. Sprinkle with paprika. Cook about 4 inches from moderately hot coals for 8 minutes. Baste with sauce and sprinkle with paprika. Turn and cook for 7 to 10 minutes longer or until fish flakes easily when tested with a fork.

DEVILED SCROD
Serves 4

1½ to 2 pounds scrod
  (small haddock or cod)
¼ cup chopped green pepper
¼ cup minced onion
1 tablespoon prepared mustard
1 teaspoon Worcestershire sauce

1/8 teaspoon tabasco sauce
3½ tablespoons lemon juice
½ cup butter
2 cups fine, soft bread crumbs
2 tablespoons grated Parmesan cheese

Wipe scrod with a damp cloth; cut into 4 portions. Combine green pepper, onion, mustard, Worcestershire sauce, tabasco sauce, and lemon juice. Melt butter, stir in bread crumbs; add to vegetable mixture, blending well. Season scrod with salt and pepper; dot with additional butter. Place on foil-lined broiler rack with surface about 4 inches below source of heat. Broil 5 minutes. Remove from broiler. Turn scrod; top with bread mixture. Return to broiler. Broil 5 to 7 minutes, or until fish flakes easily. Sprinkle with Parmesan cheese. Broil 1 minute longer.

POACHED

POACHED FISH

Poaching fish retains its moisture without losing the flavor. The fish is cooked in liquid kept just below boiling. The liquid is often used to make a sauce.

FISH FILLETS WITH LEMON PARSLEY SAUCE

8 fish fillets
juice of a large lemon
1½ cups water
1 bay leaf

1 teaspoon grated lemon rind
1 tablespoon choped parsley
½ cup margarine

Immerse fillets in lemon juice. Remove, reserving juice, and roll as for jelly roll. Fasten with toothpicks. Place fillet rolls in shallow pan holding two inches water (about 1½ cups) and a bay leaf. Bring to a slow boil for thirty seconds. Reduce heat to simmer and cover. Simmer five minutes or until tender. While fillets are cooking combine ½ cup margarine with the lemon juice in a saucepan. Add parsley and lemon rind to make a sauce. Place cooked fillets on a hot platter. Remove toothpicks and pour sauce over fish.

FILLET OF SOLE IN GALLIANO BUTTER
Serves 6

2 pounds fillet or sole or
    flounder
2/3 cup whole or slivered
    blanched almonds
2/3 cup butter

¼ cup Liquore Galliano
¼ cup lemon juice
¼ cup chopped parsley
salt
pepper

To make Galliano butter, in a large skillet or chafing dish, saute almonds in butter until slightly toasted. Allow butter to brown, then stir in Galliano, lemon juice, parsley and seasonings. Add sole fillets. Cover and cook over medium heat 7 to 10 minutes, until fish flakes easily. Spoon Galliano butter over fish frequently as it cooks.

55

HADDOCK FILLETS WITH CHEESE SAUCE
Serves 4

2 pounds haddock fillets
½ cup white wine
1 cup water
1 small bay leaf
pinch of thyme
2 taplespoons parsley, chopped

2 tablespoons shallots, finely chopped
1 pound cooked fresh spinach or
one medium sized can spinach
½ pound sharp or mild cheese, shredded or grated
¼ cup grated cheese

Place haddock fillets in a shallow pan with just enough water to cover. Add wine, 1 cup water, bay leaf, thyme, parsley and shallots. Simmer 5 minutes. Remove fillets and place on a bed of cooked spinach in an ovenproof dish. Pour cheese sauce, made by adding ½ pound cheese to poaching liquid, over the fillets. Sprinkle with grated cheese. Glaze under the broiler and serve.

WATER-BROILED FISH FILLETS WITH BUTTER-EGG SAUCE
Serves 4 -5
No broiler mess to clean up and fish is guaranteed not to dry out, burn, overcook or cook unevenly.

1½ pounds fresh fillet of haddock
boiling water
salt and pepper
paprika

¼ cup butter or margarine, melted
2 hard boiled eggs, chopped
chopped parsley or dill

Rinse fish quickly under running cold water and drain on paper towels. Cut in 4 or 5 portions and arrange, skin side down, in 11"x7" baking pan. (Not glass). Fold tail parts double so all portions are of same thickness. Pour boiling water over fish to half the level of thickness of fish. Sprinkle with salt, pepper and paprika. Broil about 3" from heat for 12 minutes or until fish is opaque and flakes easily with fork. Remove fish from broth and serve with heated mixture of ¼ cup fish broth, the butter and eggs. Garnish with parsley or dill.

FINNAN HADDIE

2 pounds finnan haddie (dried,
smoked haddock)
1½ cups milk
¼ pound butter, melted

1 cup heavy cream
4 hard boiled eggs, sliced
black pepper

Poach finnan haddie fillets in milk until fish flakes easily. Flake fish and combine fish and poaching liquid with ¼ pound butter in saucepan. Add cream, eggs, and black pepper (to taste). Blend thoroughly.

POLLOCK FILLETS FLORENTINE
Serves 6

2 pounds pollock fillets
1½ cups hot water
6 tablespoons lemon juice
1 teaspoon salt
1 small bay leaf
1 small (2½") onion, thinly sliced
1 package (2 ounce) prepared white sauce mix
1 cup milk
¼ teaspoon nutmeg

dash cayenne
4 slices bacon, diced
2 tablespoons bacon drippings
2 packages (10 ounce) frozen leaf spinach or broccoli, cooked and drained
½ cup shredded American or Swiss cheese or ¼ cup shredded Parmesan cheese

Cut fish fillets into 6 equal portions. Combine water, 2 tablespoons lemon juice, salt, bay leaf and onion in 10" fry pan. Bring to a boil. Add fish. Cover and simmer until fish flakes easily when tested with a fork. (About 10 minutes) Prepare sauce mix as directed, using milk instead of water. Stir 2 tablespoons lemon juice, nutmeg and cayenne into sauce. Set aside. Fry bacon until crisp. Remove pieces from pan and save. Save 2 tablespoons bacon drippings. Combine well drained spinach or broccoli, 2 tablespoons lemon juice, bacon and the bacon drippings. Arrange vegetable in even layer in shallow 2 quart baking dish. Place fish portions on vegetable. Pour sauce over fish. Sprinkle with cheese. Broil about 4" from heat until cheese melts and browns slightly.

PESCE ROSSE (OCEAN PERCH)
OR MERLUZZO A BIANCO (WHITING)
Serves 4

6 small whiting or ocean perch
2½ cups water
6 cloves garlic, chopped
½ cup parsley

1 tablespoon lemon juice
oil
pinch saffron

Lightly brown chopped garlic in oil. Add water, parsley, and saffron. Cover and simmer for 10 minutes. Add fish and cook for 10 more minutes. Add lemon juice just before serving. Italian bread and white wine are often served with this dish. The bread is dunked in the poaching liquid before eating.

SAUCES
STUFFINGS

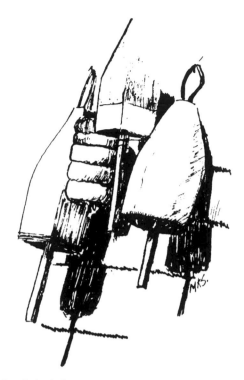

To enhance the flavor of the simpler fish dishes, try a tangy sauce. Pour the sauce over the fried, baked or broiled fish just before serving, or offer several sauces and let your guest choose his own tasty accompaniment.

SAUCE FOR FISH

2 tablespoons butter	1 tablespoon chopped parsley
1 tablespoon vinegar	½ teaspoon salt
1 teaspoon lemon juice	¼ teaspoon pepper

Place the butter in a frying pan and when it is browned add the other ingredients. Boil up once and serve. This sauce is poured over fried fish or boiled fish just before serving.

BUTTER SAUCE

½ cup butter, melted	2 hard-cooked eggs, chopped
few tablespoons fish broth	(or ¼ cup chopped green onion,
	2 tablespoons drained capers,
	or 2 tablespoons lemon juice.)

Mix all ingredients together and heat.

PARSLEY BUTTER SAUCE

3 tablespoons butter
½ to 1 tablespoon lemon juice

1 tablespoon chopped parsley
½ teaspoon salt
1/8 teaspoon pepper

Cream butter and add lemon juice, chopped parsley, salt and pepper. This may be used to spread on fried or broiled fish.

GALLIANO BUTTER

1 stick butter
1/8 teaspoon garlic powder
½ teaspoon salt

½ teaspoon pepper
½ teaspoon sweet basil
½ cup Galliano

Combine all ingredients and heat together. Spread over baked or broiled fish.

EGG SAUCE

1 tablespoon butter
1 tablespoon flour
1 cup milk
½ teaspoon salt
$\frac{1}{16}$ teaspoon ground black pepper

$\frac{1}{16}$ teaspoon onion powder
2 large hard-cooked eggs, diced
2 teaspoons lemon juice

Melt butter and stir in flour. Gradually add milk along with salt, pepper, and onion powder. Stir and cook until slightly thickened. Add eggs and lemon juice.

MUSHROOM-ALMOND SAUCE

1 can (10½ ounce) condensed
   cream of mushroom soup
½ cup cooked peas

¼ cup slivered toasted almonds

Combine ingredients and heat well.

WHITE SAUCE

2 tablespoons butter
2 tablespoons flour

½ cup milk
salt and pepper

In double boiler top or small heavy pan melt butter and stir in flour. Blend over low heat and slowly stir in milk. Stir constantly and bring slowly to the boiling point. Cook 2 minutes and season with salt and pepper to taste.

CHEESE SAUCE

1 cup white sauce   2 tablespoons sherry
3/4 cup cheddar cheese

Combine all ingredients, mixing well.

CREAMY SAUCE

2 cups medium white sauce   prepared mustard or
  (prepare with part milk   horseradish,
  and part fish broth)   Lemon juice, curry powder,
                      hard cooked egg

Mix sauce and seasoning to taste.

EGG AND CHIVE SAUCE

2 cups well-seasoned   3 hard-cooked eggs
  white sauce   1 tablespoon cut chives
1 tablespoon grated onion   1 tablespoon diced pimiento

While the butter for white sauce is melting, add the grated onion. After white sauce is made add eggs, sliced, and the chives and pimiento.

CAPER SAUCE

1 cup yogurt   2 tablespoons instant
2 tablespoons chopped capers   minced onion
1 tablespoon lemon juice   1 teaspoon grated lemon
1 tablespoon chopped parsley   rind

Combine ingredients and mix thoroughly. Chill.

TARTAR SAUCE

½ cup mayonnaise   2 teaspoons finely
2 tablespoons finely chopped   grated onion
  sweet pickles   ½ teaspoon Worcester-
1 tablespoon minced parsley   shire sauce

Mix ingredients in a jar and after stirring sauce thoroughly shake the jar until it is well mixed. Cover and refrigerate for flavors to blend. (If you use savory, add a pinch to your tartar sauce for a little different flavor.)

SECOND TARTAR SAUCE

1 cup mayonnaise
1 tablespoon chopped capers
1 tablespoon chopped green
  olives

1 tablespoon chopped mixed
  sweet pickles
1 tablespoon chopped parsley
½ teaspoon paprika

Combine ingredients, mixing well.

HOMEMADE TARTAR SAUCE

½ cup mayonnaise
2 tablespoons minced parsley
2 tablespoons minced sweet gherkins

1½ tablespoons lemon juice
1 tablespoon minced onion

Combine ingredients, mixing well. Chill

LEMON-MAYONNAISE SAUCE

¼ cup mayonnaise
2 tablespoons lemon juice

1 teaspoon minced onion
dash tabasco sauce

Combine ingredients and mix well.

FESTIVAL SAUCE

1 cup mayonnaise
2 tablespoons grated onion
¼ cup chili sauce
dash tabasco sauce

2 tablespoons snipped parsley
1 tablespoon pimiento
⅓ cup dairy sour cream

Combine all ingredients except sour cream. Chill several hours. Just before
serving, fold in sour cream.

HORSERADISH SAUCE

⅓ cup mayonnaise
¼ cup minced dill pickle
2 tablespoons horseradish

1 tablespoon milk
dash pepper

Combine all ingredients, mixing well. Refrigerate. Makes about 3/4 cup sauce.

SAUCE FOR FAVORITE FISH

2 tablespoons olive oil
1/8 teaspoon garlic powder
¼ teaspoon tabasco
2 teaspoons lemon juice

1 teaspoon sweet basil
½ teaspoon oregano
½ teaspoon salt
¼ teaspoon black pepper

Combine all ingredients and spread over fish.

SPECIAL SAUCE

4 large tomatoes, cubed
4 cloves of garlic, mashed
½ cup parsley, chopped

2 lemons, squeezed
½ cup oil
salt and pepper

Place ingredients in a large bowl and marinate for one hour. Broil fish to charcoal flavor. Lightly salt fish. Place on serving platter. Pour sauce over hot broiled fish.

GREEN SAUCE

Finely chopped watercress,
    chives, parsley, dill,
spinach, green onion to taste

1 small dill pickle, chopped
2/3 cup mayonnaise
⅓ cup dairy sour cream

Mix all ingredients together. Makes about 1-1½ cups. Keeps well in refrigerator. Good with broiled and fried fish.

FOO YUNG SAUCE

2 chicken boullion cubes
½ teaspoon sugar
2 cups water

2 tablespoons cornstarch
2 tablespoons soy sauce

Dissolve boullion cubes and sugar in boiling water. Combine cornstarch and soy sauce and add to boullion mixture. Cook until thick and clear, stirring constantly.

CUCUMBER, DILL, AND CAPER SAUCE

1 cup diced, seeded cucumber
½ cup water
2 tablespoons butter
2 tablespoons flour
2 teaspoons lemon juice

1 teaspoon grated lemon peel
1 teaspoon grated onion
½ teaspoon salt
few grains of pepper
1 tablespoon fresh chopped dill
1 tablespoon capers

Cook cucumber in water until tender and clear. Drain and measure cooking water; add enough water to make 1 cup. Melt butter and blend in flour. Add cooking water mixture; stir until smooth and thickened. Add lemon juice, lemon peel, onion, salt, pepper, dill, capers, and the cooked cucumbers. Heat to serving temperature.

LOBSTER SAUCE

3 tablespoons butter
3 tablespoons flour
⅓ cup fish stock
1 tall can (1-2/3 cups)
    evaporated milk
3/4 teaspoon salt

dash tabasco sauce
½ teaspoon nutmeg
1 cup fresh lobster
    meat
(optional—3 tablespoons
    dry sherry)

Melt butter; blend in flour. Add fish stock and milk. Heat over medium heat until smooth and thickened. Stir in salt, tabasco sauce and nutmeg. Add diced lobster meat. Just before serving add sherry and heat to serving temperature. Garnish with parsley.

SHRIMP SAUCE

½ cup catsup
3 tablespoons lemon juice
1 tablespoon horseradish
5 or 6 drops tabasco sauce

¼ teaspoon salt
2 teaspoons Worcestershire sauce
a little celery salt

Mix together well.

SEAFOOD SAUCE

½ cup chili sauce
⅓ cup prepared horseradish
¼ teaspoon salt
1/8 teaspoon pepper

⅓ cup ketchup
1½ teaspoons Worcestershire sauce
2 tablespoons lemon juice
¼ cup minced celery

Combine all ingredients. Place in a jar and keep covered and chill. Makes about 1½ cups.

COCKTAIL SAUCE

⅓ cup chili sauce
⅓ cup catsup
1 teaspoon minced onion
2 teaspoons tarragon vinegar
¼ teaspoon salt

1 tablespoon lemon juice
few drops tabasco
¼ to ½ teaspoon sugar
1 small clove garlic

Combine above ingredients and chill. Remove garlic before serving.

MARINARA SAUCE FOR SHRIMP

1 clove garlic, minced
2 tablespoons olive oil
2½ cups canned pressed and drained
   whole or Italian tomatoes

6 anchovies, finely chopped
½ teaspoon oregano
1 tablespoon parsley, chopped

Saute garlic lightly in olive oil plus oil from anchovies. Slowly add tomatoes, then stir in anchovies, oregano, and parsley. Bring to a boil, then reduce heat and simmer uncovered 15-20 minutes, stirring occasionally.

Saute until white, 1 pound peeled raw shrimp in 1 tablespoon salted oil. Add to marinara sauce and simmer 7 minutes. May be served on macaroni or spaghetti.

HERB CREAM SAUCE FOR BREADED SHRIMP

1 cup sour cream
3 tablespoons chopped chives
2 tablespoons chopped parsley

2 tablespoons prepared
   horseradish
salt and pepper to taste

Combine all ingredients; mix well. Chill thoroughly. Makes about 1¼ cups.

CURRY CAPER SAUCE FOR BREADED SHRIMP

½ cup mayonnaise
1 tablespoon capers

1 teaspoon curry powder

Combine all ingredients; mix well. Makes about ½ cup.

SPICY BARBECUE SAUCE

3/4 cup chopped onion
½ cup salad oil
3/4 cup catsup
3/4 cup water
⅓ cup lemon juice
2 teaspoons salt

3 tablespoons sugar
3 tablespoons Worcestershire
   sauce
2 tablespoons prepared mustard
½ teaspoon pepper

Saute onion in salad oil until tender, but not brown. Add remaining ingredients and mix well.

PEPPY SEAFOOD SAUCE

½ cup ketchup
½ cup chili sauce
3 tablespoons lemon juice
1 tablespoon horseradish
1 tablespoon mayonnaise
dash pepper

1 teaspoon Worcestershire sauce
½ teaspoon grated onion
¼ teaspoon salt
3 drops liquid hot pepper
   sauce

Combine all ingredients; chill. Makes about 1½ cups. Serves 6.

TOMATO BREAD STUFFING

¼ cup finely chopped onion
¼ cup finely chopped celery
¼ cup butter or margarine
2 cups soft bread cubes
¼ teaspoon salt

¼ teaspoon thyme, mint or
   poultry seasoning
few grains pepper
1 tomato, chopped

Cook onion and celery in melted butter or margarine for about 5 minutes or until tender. Remove from heat and combine with bread cubes. Add seasonings and tomato. Mix thoroughly. Makes about 2⅓ cups stuffing. The addition of tomato to this standard bread stuffing mixture adds a nice color and flavor accent. Keep it in mind for a small cod, haddock or other white-fleshed fish.

MADOULEE STUFFING

¼ cup finely chopped onion
¼ cup finely chopped celery
3 tablespoons butter or
   margarine

1 cup soft bread cubes
3/4 cup shredded carrot
½ teaspoon salt
few grains pepper

Cook onion and celery in melted butter or margarine until tender but not browned. Remove from heat. Add bread cubes, carrot and seasonings. Mix thoroughly. Makes 1¼ cups stuffing.

FRUIT STUFFING

2 cups whole wheat bread,
   cubed
1 apple, chopped
3/4 cup raisins
½ teaspoon thyme, chopped

1 teaspoon parsley, chopped
1 onion chopped
1 egg
3 tablespoons butter

Saute onion in butter. Add remaining ingredients, and toss until well moistened. If desired additional types of fruit such as dried apricots or peaches may be added or substituted.

RICE STUFFING

3 cups cooked brown rice
¼ cup diced celery
¼ cup minced onion
¼ cup diced green pepper
½ cup sliced mushrooms
¼ cup butter or margarine

1 teaspoon salt
1/8 teaspoon pepper
¼ teaspoon tarragon
¼ teaspoon marjoram
¼ to ½ cup fish stock or
    water

Cook diced vegetables in butter or margarine until tender. Add mushrooms, seasonings and stock or water. Simmer 5 minutes. Combine with rice and mix thoroughly. Is enough to stuff a large fish.

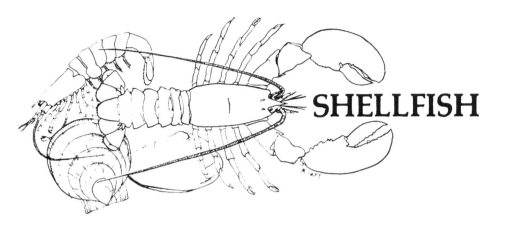

SHELLFISH

BOILED LOBSTER

Using a 12 - 14 quart kettle, boil 6 inches of water. Into this put ¼ cup salt. Let come to a boil again and drop in lobster, head first; reduce to medium heat. Boil 12 minutes for a one pound lobster, 15 - 18 minutes for a 1½ pound lobster and 20 - 22 minutes for a 2 pound lobster. The shell will be bright red when done. Transfer to a warm platter and serve with lots of melted butter.

Parts not usually eaten in the body itself but are delicious are the roe, which is an orangish yellow mass and the tomale which is a gray green paste. Many small pieces of meat are found in the cavity, not just in the tails and claws.

BROILED LIVE LOBSTER

Allow one small or ½ large lobster per person.

Put the lobster on its back and make a deep, sharp cut through the entire length of the body and tail with a heavy sharp-pointed knife or lobster shears. Spread open and remove the black line and the stomach. Crack the claw shells with a mallet.

Place in the broiler, shell side down. Sprinkle with olive oil or melted butter. Broil slowly about 20 minutes or until the flesh is lightly browned. Serve with melted butter.

BAKED STUFFED LOBSTER
Serves 2

2 1½ pound lobsters
4 cups cracker crumbs
(Ritz, Hi Ho etc.)
1½ cups melted butter

½ teaspoon garlic powder
lobster liver (tomale)

Add melted butter to cracker crumbs and garlic powder. Split two lobsters removing vein and stomach. Save livers and add to cracker crumb mixture. Stuff lobsters with mixture. Bake at 450° F for 20 minutes.

LOBSTER NEWBURG
Serves 4

3 tablespoons margarine
3 tablespoons flour
½ teaspoon salt
1½ cups milk
2 cups cooked, chopped
lobster pieces

1 cup sliced celery
2 tablespoons chili sauce
2 teaspoons lemon juice
dash paprika
parsley or olive slices

Melt butter or margarine in saucepan. Blend in flour and salt. Remove from heat. Gradually add milk, stirring until mixture is smooth. Cook over medium heat, stirring constantly, until mixture comes to a boil. Reduce heat and simmer 1 minute. Add lobster, celery, chili sauce, lemon juice and paprika. Heat. Serve over rice. Garnish with sprigs of parsley or olive slices.

TOASTED LOBSTER SANDWICH

Meat from 2-pound lobster
or ½ pound canned lobster
1 egg yolk
few drops onion juice
¼ teaspoon salt
⅛ teaspoon paprika
few grains pepper

3 tablespoons butter
½ can mushrooms
3 tablespoons flour
½ cup milk
½ cup cream
1 egg yolk
stale bread slices
1 cup grated cheese

Chop lobster meat and add 1 egg yolk, onion juice, salt, paprika and pepper. Remove crusts from bread and cut into strips ½ inch wide. Spread with lobster mixture. Melt butter in skillet, and saute mushrooms for five minutes. Add flour, blending well, then add the milk and cream. Stir mixture until it boils and add egg yolk. Cool slightly then pour sauce over lobster. Sprinkle with grated cheese and bake in hot oven (400°) about 10 minutes.

STEAMED CLAMS
Serves 6

About 1 hour before serving: In cold water, with vegetable brush, scrub 6 dozen soft-shelled clams; rinse in water until free of sand. Place clams into steamer, or on rack in large kettle with 1 cup boiling water (or enough to cover bottom). Cover kettle with tight-fitting lid and steam over low heat just until clams open, 5 to 10 minutes. Serve clams in soup bowls with individual cups of butter. Pour broth into mugs and sprinkle with a little chopped parsley. To eat: With fingers, pull clams from shells by the neck; dip first in broth to remove any sand, then into butter. All except the tough skin of the neck may be eaten. When sand settles to the bottom, the broth may be drunk.

FRIED CLAMS
Serves 6

Vegetable oil for deep
  frying
3 eggs
1 cup milk
1 cup flour

3 cups drained shucked,
  soft shell or long-neck clams
salt
Lemon wedges

Preheat oven to its lowest setting. Line a large cookie sheet with double thickness of paper towels and place it in the oven. Pour vegetable oil into a deep frying or large heavy saucepan to a depth of about 3 inches and heat until oil is 375°F on a deep frying thermometer. In a bowl, beat the eggs until well blended, then stir in the milk. Spread the flour in a large strip of wax paper. Drop the clams into the egg-milk mixture and let them soak for a minute. Pick up a handfull of the soaked clams, roll them in the flour until well coated. Immediately drop the floured clams into the hot oil and deep-fry for 1 - 2 minutes, until they are golden brown. As they brown, transfer them to the towel-lined pan and keep them warm in the oven while the rest are cooked. Serve with ketchup or tartar sauce.

CLAMBURGERS

2 cans chopped clams, drained
1 egg well beaten
1 cup cracker crumbs.

1 teaspoon salt
¼ teaspoon pepper

Combine ingredients in the above order, and mix well. Form round cakes and fry in ½ cup hot fat or cooking oil. (Tartar sauce goes well with these also).

BAKED STUFFED SHRIMP
Serves 2

6 jumbo or ¾ pound native
   shrimp
cracker crumbs (Ritz, Hi Ho, etc.)
½ pound butter, lightly salted
1 cup mushrooms, sliced

1 teaspoon parsley flakes
¼ teaspoon garlic salt
¼ teaspoon celery salt
½ cup milk
1 teaspoon Parmesan cheese

Saute mushrooms in butter. Add milk and bring to a boil. Remove from heat and add cracker crumbs, parsley, and seasonings to mixture. Mix well. Place on well cleaned, deveined shrimp so as to cover the entire opening of shrimp. Bake for 20 minutes in 350° oven. Serve with cream butter.

CURRIED SHRIMP
Serves 4

¼ cup butter
1 tablespoon curry powder
1 medium onion, chopped
3-4 tablespoons flour
1½ cups milk

1 teaspoon salt
⅛ teaspoon ginger
1 pound cooked shrimp
1 avocado cooked and diced
2 cups hot cooked rice

In a saucepan heat butter, stir in curry powder and onion; simmer a few minutes. Add flour and stir until smooth. Add milk slowly. Stir and cook until thickened and smooth. Blend in salt and ginger. Add shrimp and heat through. Fold in diced avocado and serve over hot fluffy rice.

SCALLOPED SHRIMP
Serves 6

4 tablespoons butter
2 tablespoons minced onions
1 tablespoon minced green pepper
4 tablespoons flour

½ teaspoon dry mustard
2 cups milk
2 cups cooked shrimp
1 cup buttered bread crumbs

Melt butter and cook onions and green pepper in it until tender. Blend in flour and mustard. Add milk and cook until thickened, stirring constantly. Add shrimp. Pour into greased casserole, cover with buttered crumbs and bake in moderate over (350°F) about 20 minutes.

SPAGHETTI WITH SHRIMP SAUCE
Serves 4 - 6

1 dozen fresh shrimp, cooked
   or a 5-ounce can shrimp
4 tablespoons olive or salad oil
¼ teaspoon oregano

1 teaspoon minced parsley
1 pint marinara sauce
1 pound spaghetti
grated cheese

Saute drained shrimp for a few moments in oil with oregano and parsley. Add sauce and simmer for 8 to 10 minutes. Serve over cooked spaghetti with grated cheese.

MUSHROOM AND SHRIMP DELIGHT
Serves 4

1 pound shrimp, shelled
   deveined and cooked
1 cup long-grain rice
1 6-ounce can sliced
   mushrooms, drained
1 4½-ounce jar strained
   apricots
lemon wedges for garnish

¼ cup sour cream
1½ tablespoons butter or
   margarine, melted
3/4 teaspoon salt
1/8 teaspoon pepper
parsley for garnish

About 1 hour before serving: Preheat oven to 350°F. Cook rice as label directs. In well-greased 1½ quart casserole, combine rice with shrimp and remaining ingredients except garnishes. Toss gently until mixed. Cover and bake 40 minutes. Garnish with parsley and lemon.

SHRIMP-RICE PARISIEN
Serves 4

1½ pounds cooked shrimp
½ cup butter
1 clove garlic, crushed
2 tablespoons cooking sherry

3 tablespoons bread crumbs
2 tablespoons chopped chives
2 teaspoons chopped parsley
½ teaspoon paprika

In a large skillet melt parsley and stir in garlic, bread crumbs, chives, sherry, parsley and paprika. Add cooked shrimp; cook over low heat 10 - 15 minutes. Serve over hot buttered rice.

SHRIMP AND SCALLOP SKILLET
Serves 4

1 4-ounce can sliced mushrooms,
   drained
1 can frozen condensed cream
   of shrimp soup
2-3 cups cut-up, cooked
   shrimp and scallops

1 tablespoon butter or
   margarine
½ cup light cream
3 tablespoons sauterne wine

Brown mushrooms lightly in butter. Add soup and cream; heat slowly until soup is thawed. Blend in seafood. Heat, stirring often. Add sauterne just before serving.

HAWAIIAN SHRIMP SALAD
Serves 4

1 pound cooked shrimp
1 cucumber, cubed
1 green pepper seeded and diced
1 cup pineapple, drained and
    cubed

½ cup salted peanuts
1 cup real mayonnaise
⅓ cup dairy sour cream
½ teaspoon dry mustard
Salt, pepper, lemon juice
    to taste

Toss all ingredients together and chill. Heap in halved and hollowed pineapple shells or on crisp lettuce.

"SOUPER" SHRIMP CANOES
Serves 6 - 8

1 can (10½ ounces) condensed
    cream of celery soup
1½ pounds cleaned shrimp, cooked
    and cut up (3 cups)
½ cup chopped green pepper
½ cup sliced ripe olives

1 tablespoon lemon juice
1/8 teaspoon tarragon
2 dashes hot pepper sauce
6 to 8 round hard rolls
lettuce
lemon slices

Combine all ingredients except rolls, lettuce and lemon slices. Chill if desired. Cut slice from top of each roll. Hollow out leaving ½ inch thick shell. Line with lettuce; fill with shrimp mixture. Garnish with lemon slices.

SCALLOPS EN BROCHETTE
Serves 4

1 pound sea scallops
    (about 12)
12 small mushrooms
½ large green pepper
2 tablespoons melted
    butter or margarine
2 tablespoons lemon juice

1 tablespoon salad oil
½ teaspoon salt
dash pepper
4 slices bacon
4 slices processed cheddar cheese
4 thick lemon wedges

About 1 hour and 15 minutes before serving: Remove stems from mushrooms. (Refrigerate stems for use in soup another day.) Cut green pepper into 8 pieces about 1 inch square. In pie plate, combine butter, lemon juice, oil, salt and pepper. Add scallops, mushrooms and green pepper pieces; cover, refrigerate 30 minutes, tossing occasionally. Preheat broiler. In medium skillet over medium-high heat, fry bacon until brown but still limp; drain on paper towels. Run a skewer through one end of a bacon slice and then lace bacon between ¼ of the scallops, mushrooms, and green pepper pieces. Repeat with 3 more skewers. Place skewers on broiling pan and broil 10 minutes, turning frequently. Cut cheese slices into fourths. When skewered food is done, place cheese strips on top of skewers, overlapping if necessary. Broil until cheese melts.

CHARCOAL BROILED SCALLOPS
Serves 4

2 pounds scallops, fresh or
  frozen
½ cup oil
¼ cup lemon juice

2 teaspoons salt
¼ teaspoon white pepper
½ pound sliced bacon
paprika

Thaw scallops, if frozen. Rinse with cold water to remove any shell particles. Place scallops in a bowl. Combine oil, lemon juice, salt and pepper. Pour sauce over scallops and let stand for 30 minutes, stirring occasionally. Cut each slice of bacon in half lengthwise then crosswise. Remove scallops, reserving sauce for basting. Wrap each scallop in a piece of bacon and fasten with a toothpick. Place scallops in well-greased, hinged, wire grills. Sprinkle with paprika. Cook about 4 inches from moderately hot coals for 5 minutes. Baste with sauce and sprinkle with paprika. Turn and cook for 5 to 7 minutes longer, or until bacon is crisp.

SCALLOPS NEW ENGLAND
Serves 4

36 sea scallops
  (about 3 pounds)
½ cup butter
2 tablespoons minced onion
3 tablespoons minced lettuce
2 tablespoons minced celery

3 tablespoons dry bread crumbs
¼ teaspoon herb blend for fish
½ teaspoon anchovy paste
¼ teaspoon salt
dash pepper

Melt 5 tablespoons butter; add all ingredients except scallops and mix well. Heat carefully, do not let butter brown. Place scallops on foil-lined broiler pan, dot with remaining butter. Broil until lightly browned. Place 6 scallops in each of 6 scallop shells. Scatter crumb mixture all over. Broil until heated thoroughly. Serve at once.

SCALLOPS PORTUGUESE
Serves 4

1 pound scallops
¼ cup butter
1 garlic clove, minced

¼ teaspoon salt
½ cup chopped parsley
dash pepper

Cut large scallops in half, pat dry with paper toweling. Melt butter. Add garlic and salt, cook until garlic is golden brown. Add scallops and cook 5 to 7 minutes, stirring often. Sprinkle with freshly ground pepper. Add freshly chopped parsley and cook 1 minute longer. Serve hot.

FRIED SCALLOPS
Serves 4

1 pound scallops
1 egg, beaten

1 cup crushed cracker crumbs
or fine bread crumbs

Cover the scallops with boiling water and let them stand 3 minutes; drain and dry with paper towels, dip in egg, then crumbs and fry in hot oil until brown. (Or, bake 15 minutes at 450°, turning to brown).

SCALLOP CAKES
Serves 4

1 pint of scallops
2 eggs
2 cups flour

2 teaspoons baking powder
milk
salt and pepper

Parboil scallops in very little water; drain and chop very fine. Beat eggs slightly, add flour sifted with baking powder. Mix with enough milk to make a batter that will drop easily from a spoon. Beat well together and add scallops. Heat ½ cup cooking oil in frying pan and drop batter by spoonfuls into the hot oil. Sprinkle with seasonings. Brown and turn to brown on the other side.

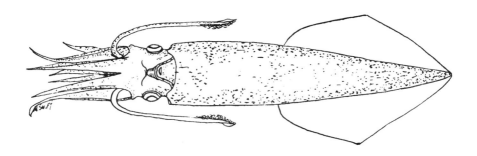

DELICACIES

MORE FOOD FROM THE SEA

There are many unusual and inexpensive species of fish which the adventurous cook can try. Already enjoyed as delicacies in Europe and the Far East, many of these fish have recently become known on Cape Ann. Your favorite fish dealer should be able to order these delicacies for you, for in most cases, the fish is more plentiful than the market for it.

SALTWATER CATFISH

The North Atlantic catfish produces delicious fillets, and is not to be confused with the fresh water catfish. It can be used as a substitute for haddock or other whitefish in any recipe. Here is a special recipe that makes catfish taste like lobster!

MOCK LOBSTERS
Serves 2 - 3

1 lb. catfish
2 tablespoons mayonnaise
1 tablespoon milk

10-12 Ritz or HI HO cracker crumbs
Grated cheese to taste
Dabs of butter

Coat catfish with mixture of milk and mayonnaise. Coat both sides with cracker crumbs and sprinkle top with grated cheese and butter. Bake 20 minutes at 375°F.

How to clean squid

To clean squid, grasp head and mantle (body) firmly in hands and pull off head, tentacles and ink sac. Pull transparent backbone or quill from the mantle. Squeeze any remaining entrails from inside of mantle. Hold under cold running water, peel off speckled membrane that covers the mantle. Wash mantle thoroughly, inside and out and slice according to recipe.

JOLLY SQUID
Serves 3 - 4

2 pounds whole squid, fresh or frozen (approximately 8 medium or 14 small squid)
Rice-Potato Stuffing (below)

1 can (1 pound) tomatoes
2 tablespoons grated Italian cheese (Romano or Parmesan)

Clean squid. Chop tentacles for stuffing. Stuff squid loosely. Close opening with small skewer or toothpick. Place squid in a single layer in a well-greased baking dish approximately 12 x 8 x 2 inches. Place the tomatoes on top of squid. Sprinkle with cheese. Cover with aluminum foil. Bake in a moderate oven 350°F, for 30 to 45 minutes or until squid are tender.

Rice Potato Stuffing

¼ cup chopped onion
¼ cup cooking or olive oil
1 cup rice, cooked
½ cup shredded raw potatoes
2 tablespoons grated Italian cheese (Romano or Parmesan)

2 tablespoons chopped parsley
Chopped tentacles
1 egg, beaten
½ teaspoon salt
Dash pepper

Cook onion in hot oil until tender. Add tentacles and cook for 3 to 5 minutes. Add rice, potatoes, cheese, parsley, egg, salt and pepper. Mix thoroughly. Makes approximately 1½ cups stuffing.

SQUID SALAD RINGS

2 pounds whole squid
   fresh or frozen
1 quart boiling water
1 tablespoon salt
1 clove garlic, crushed

1 bay leaf
1 cup diced celery
⅓ cup sliced green olives
3/4 cup Italian dressing
paprika to taste

Clean squid. Add salt, garlic, bay leaf and squid to boiling water. Cover and simmer for 10 to 15 minutes or until squid are tender. Drain and rinse in cold water. Drain. Cut mantle into ¼ inch rings. Cut tentacles into ½ inch pieces. Combine celery, olives, Italian dressing and squid. Cover and let stand for several hours in the refrigerator. Sprinkle with paprika. Makes approximately 2½ cups salad. Serve as an appetizer.

SQUID SWEET SOUR STYLE
Serves 3 - 4

2 pounds whole squid,
   fresh or frozen
1 cup chopped celery
1 cup chopped onion
¼ cup cooking or olive oil
2 tablespoons drained capers

¼ cup tomato paste
¼ cup cider vinegar
1 tablespoon sugar
½ teaspoon salt
1/8 teaspoon pepper

Clean squid. Cut mantle into 1 inch strips. Cut tentacles into 1 inch pieces. Cook celery and onion in hot oil until tender. Add squid. Cover and simmer for 5 minutes. Rince and drain capers. Add capers, tomato paste, vinegar, sugar, salt and pepper. Cover and simmer for approximately 20 minutes or until squid are tender, stirring occasionally.

BAKED SQUID

Dip pieces of squid in oil, then in Fiesta bread crumb mixture. (see page 33). In the center of each piece, place a strip of American or provolone cheese, some chopped mushrooms and some stewed tomatoes. Roll up. Place in a baking dish and cover with foil. Bake at 375° for 30 minutes.

EEL ITALIAN STYLE
Serves 6

2½ pounds of eel cut into chunks
salt and pepper
cooking oil
2 tablespoons chopped onion
1 teaspoon chopped shallots (optional)
¼ pound of mushrooms diced small

⅓ cup white wine
3/4 cup tomato sauce
chopped parsley, chervil,
    and tarragon

Season the eel chunks with salt and pepper and fry briskly in oil for a short time, just enough to stiffen the fish. Remove from the pan and in the same oil, brown the chopped onion. When the onion is nearly done, add a teaspoon of chopped shallots, and the mushrooms. Put the eel back in the pan, add the white wine and three-quarters of a cup of tomato sauce. Simmer, with lid on, for half an hour. Place in a shallow platter, sprinkle with chopped parsley, chervil, and tarragon.

EEL EL GRECCO (GREEK STYLE)
Serves 6

2 pounds of eel, skinned, cut into
    two inch pieces
¼ cup olive oil
a pinch of thyme leaves

½ lemon (juice of it)
lemon slices
parsley

Sprinkle blended salt and pepper over the pieces of eel. Heat the olive oil in a baking dish. Add the garlic and thyme. Place the eel in this hot mixture, squeeze a little lemon juice over it, and bake in a moderate over (375°) for 25 to 30 minutes. Garnish with lemon slices and parsley.

EEL AMERICAN STYLE

Eels, cut approximately two inches thick
fine breadcrumbs
salt

Skin and clean eels. Roll sliced eel pieces in fine breadcrumbs and place on grill over charcoal fire. Salt them as they grill. Serve with. a brown sauce with mustard.

SECOND EDITION BONUS

MORE RECIPIES FROM
THE FISHERMEN'S WIVES

GERRI'S FAVORITE BAKED HADDOCK
Serves 6

3 pounds haddock fillets cut
   into 3- to 4- inch pieces
2 cups crushed Ritz or Hi-Ho
   crackers
¼ cup grated Italian cheese

¼ cup finely chopped celery
⅛ teaspoon garlic powder
1 stick melted butter or margarine

Place haddock in shallow baking dish or individual sizzle dishes. Add a little water and butter to the bottom of the dish. Set aside and mix all other ingredients until well blended. Spread mixture generously over fish. Bake 400° for 20 minutes. Serve with lemon wedges and braised lettuce.

OFF SHORE BAKE
Serves 6

2 pounds fish fillets (2 pieces) cod,
   pollock, cusk or haddock
¼ cup bread crumbs
2 tablespoons grated Italian cheese
1 hard-boiled egg, sliced
1 teaspoon oregano

1 cup mashed tomatoes or tomato sauce
1 medium onion (sliced)
2 large potatoes (1 lb.) medium sliced
salt and pepper to taste
¼ cup olive oil

Oil a baking tray 14 x 10. Place 1 piece of fish in center (sprinkle with salt). Add bread crumbs on fish. Sprinkle 1 tablespoon grated cheese evenly over the fish. Place the sliced egg and about 3 tablespoons of the tomatoes. Then add oregano. Pour a little oil all over the stuffing and sprinkle 1 tablespoon of cheese. Place the other fillet on the top. Place the cut up potatoes and onion, that you have mixed together with a little salt and pepper, around the fish.

Add the tomatoes over the fish, onions and potatoes. Add the remaining oil also. Cover with foil. Bake 375° for 45 minutes until potatoes and onions are cooked.

SEAFOOD LASAGNA
Serves 8 - 10

1½ lbs.-haddock, cusk or pollock
1 lb. North Atlantic peeled shrimp
1 can 1 lb. 12 oz. tomatoes
½ cup diced onion
2 cloves garlic minced
4 tablespoons olive oil
1 small can (6 oz.) tomato paste

1½ cups shredded provolone
1 pound ricotta cheese
2 tablespoons grated Parmesan "cheese"
3 eggs
1 lb. lasagna, cooked according to
    package directions
salt and pepper to taste

Put tomatoes in blender. Blend and then strain to take out the seeds.

In a large saucepan, saute onions and garlic in olive oil. Add fish, salt and pepper. Put cover on pan and simmer until fish flakes eassily, about 7 to 10 minutes. Stir as it simmers. Add the blended tomatoes. After it comes to a boil, let it cook for 5 minutes and add can of paste and simmer 10 minutes. To thicken, the sauce should cook without the cover on.

Meanwhile in small frying pan, put a little oil. Add shrimp and cook lightly until they curl. Strain and add shrimp to fish sauce. If sauce is thick, add some of the shrimp juice and cook 5 minutes more.

Now, beat the eggs, add the ricotta and Parmesan with a little pepper to taste and mix well. Scoop about a quarter of the fish sauce and cover the bottom of a 15 x 11 x 2 inch lasagna pan. Cover with one third of the lasagna. Dot with about a third of the cheese mixture and sprinkle a third of the shredded provolone in between. Continue with layers of fish sauce, lasagna, cheeses, until you have three layers of each. Top with remaining quarter of sauce. Cover pan with aluminium foil and bake 30 minutes in 350° to 375° oven.

FISHERMAN'S KETTLE

2 pounds catfish or cusk fillets
    cut in 3-inch portions
½ cup flour with 1 teaspoon salt
1 cup oil to fry
¼ cup olive oil
1 large onion, sliced
½ celery cut in pieces

1-1 pound 12-ounce can tomatoes
    with puree
½ cup water
1 tablespoon sugar
16 capers (soak to remove salt)
⅓ cup small raisins (optional)
8 olives (green or black) cut in pieces
salt and pepper to taste

Add the salt to flour. Roll the fish in flour. Heat the oil and fry fish. Brown fish on both sides. Drain on paper and set aside.

In a kettle with olive oil, saute onions and celery until soft. Then add the tomatoes and ½ cup of water and simmer for 10 minutes. Add fish, capers, olives, raisins and sugar and cook for 20 to 30 minutes. Add salt and pepper to taste. Day-old bread is good to dunk in this meal.

BROILED FILLETS MUSHROOMS AND CHEESE
Serves 4 - 6

2 pounds fish fillets, fresh or frozen
¼ cup olive oil
1 teaspoon salt
pepper to taste

2 small cans chopped mushrooms, drained
1 cup grated mozzarella
2 tablespoons chopped parsley

Cut fillets into serving-size portions. Combine olive oil, salt and pepper. Combine mushrooms, mozzarella and parsley. Place fish on a well-greased broiler pan; brush with seasoned olive oil. Broil 3 inches from heat for 3-4 minutes. Turn carefully and brush with remaining olive oil mixture; broil 3-4 minutes longer or until fish flakes easily to the fork. Spread mushroom and mozzarella mixture on fish and broil 2-3 minutes longer or until lightly browned.

NEW ENGLAND CORNED HAKE DINNER
Serves 4

2 pounds hake
4 potatoes
3 large onions thinly sliced
1½ cups water

1 can beets, pickled or boiled or equivalent amount fresh beets
½ pound salt pork
dash pepper

Four hours before cooking, heavily salt hake and return to refrigerator. At cooking time, cut potatoes in quarters and cook until done. Dice salt pork and brown until pieces are crisp. Remove pork and saute onions in grease until transparent. Return pork scraps to onions. Cover fish with water and simmer in covered pan 10 minutes. Do not over cook. Drain fish. Arrange fish and potatoes on platter. Pour onion and pork scraps over fish and potatoes. Serve beets on side.

POOR MAN'S LOBSTER TREAT
Serves 4

1 pound Monkfish Tail, diced
½ cup bread crumbs
½ cup sliced onions
2 large cloves garlic, sliced

3 tablespoons butter
1 tablespoon grated Italian cheese
1 tablespoon green mint (cut small) or other herbs
salt and pepper to taste

In sauce pan, brown onion and garlic with butter. Add diced fish, salt and pepper and mint. Put cover on pan and simmer 5 minutes. During the 5 minutes, stir the fish. The fish turns white as it cooks.

Remove the cover and add the bread crumbs. Stir until the fish absorbs all the juice. Add cheese and cook for 3 minutes with no cover.

FISH ON THE GO

1½ pounds of fish - whiting,
   ocean perch, haddock, cheeks
   and tongues also
1½ cups water add ½ teaspoon salt
1 tablespoon chopped parsley

2 cloves of garlic mashed
1 fresh lemon
2 tablespoons olive oil

In saucepan, add the water and salt. When the water boils, add the fish. After about cooking for 5 minutes, take about half cup of water out. Add mashed garlic, parsley and oil. Cook this for 5 minutes more. Squeeze the juice from ½ lemon. Add salt and pepper to taste. Cook 3 minutes more and serve. Add the other ½ lemon juice on the serving plate.

Good to dunk crackers or bread or pour over cooked and drained spaghetti.

FRIED FISH—THE TRADITIONAL DISH

Fishermen's wives fry fish in various ways. Using 1 pound any type fish fillet:

1. Cut fish into serving pieces. Sprinkle with salt and pepper. Roll in flour and pan fry.

2. Mix ½ cup flour and ½ cup corn flour, salt and pepper. Dredge pieces of fish in mixture, dip in one beaten egg, and roll again in flour mixture. Pan fry. Makes a light puffy cutlet. Especially good for monk fish, scallops, and squid. Scallops and squid can be deep fried for crispier texture.

3. Dip cutlets in one beaten egg and roll in bread crumb mixture for Baked Fish Fiesta, p. 33. Pan fry.

4. Barbeque or broil by first dipping fish in olive oil and rolling in Baked Fish Fiesta crumb mixture. Cook on one side 10 minutes and other side 5 minutes more.

A typical meal served in the homes of fishing families is a hearty dish of spaghetti and fried fish.

FIFTH EDITION BONUS

A Special
Catch from the
Fisherman's Wife

PICKLED HERRING

1 lb. fresh filleted herring (about 6)
1 cup table salt

Put some salt in bottom of small bowl. Place fish skin down. Continue layering fish and salt finishing with a layer of salt. Put weight (dish or plate) on top and refrigerate for 4-5 days.

Wash herring well and skin. Soak in cold water 1 hour, changing 3-4 times. Cut in 1-inch pieces. Drain and pat dry.

Pickling solution

3 tablespoons water
1 teaspoon allspice
¾ cup sugar
3 large white onions, sliced
3 cups white vinegar
3 large bay leaves
dash black pepper

Boil 3 tablespoons water with 1 teaspoon allspice. Add sugar and vinegar. Mix until sugar is dissolved. In a one quart jar put 2 cups pickling solution, some onions and herring pieces, laying them and topping with onions. Fill to top with solution. Keep in tightly closed jar in refrigerator 2-3 days until ready to serve.

PICKLED HERRING BAKE
Serves 4-6

4 pickled herring, cut up in serving pieces
    (about 1½ cups herring pieces)
2 cups soft bread crumbs
¼ cup grated parmesan cheese
2 large onions, sliced thin
3 potatoes, sliced thin
¼ cup chopped parsley
pinch of salt and pepper

Saute onion until transparent. Set aside. Mix bread crumbs, cheese and parsley together. Set aside. In a greased baking pan, layer half of onions, potatoes, bread mixture and pickled herring, seasoning each layer with salt and pepper and repeating, ending with herring. Bake in oven at 375° for 30-40 minutes or until potatoes are done.

KYROUZ FISH DELIGHT
Serves 6-8

3 pounds white fish (whiting, catfish or any firm white fish)
3 tablespoons olive oil
1 medium onion, sliced thin
6 medium potatoes, cut in half
1-2 cups water, enough to cover potatoes
½ cup crushed tomato or tomato cut in pieces
1 small cabbage, sliced lengthwise into 6 pieces

In kettle, saute onion and potatoes in oil for 5 minutes, then add water, tomato, salt and pepper (to taste) and cook for 10 minutes. When potatoes are half cooked, add cabbage. When sauce comes to a boil, add fish, cover and cook for 10 minutes. *Shake* the pan—do not stir. Use bread or crackers to dunk.

GERRI'S CATCH OF THE DAY (Low Calorie)
Serves 6

1½ pounds fish (haddock, pollock, flounder or perch), cut into 6 pieces
1 lemon, sliced into 6 pieces
6 teaspoons oil
6 teaspoons butter or margarine
6 bay leaves
salt, pepper and paprika
6 pieces of aluminum foil measuring 12 × 11

Preheat oven to 400°. Lightly oil each sheet of foil using 1 teaspoon of oil per sheet. Wash and pat dry fish, place one piece in center of each piece of foil. Place 1 teaspoon of butter in center of each piece of fish. Place 1 bay leaf on each teaspoon of butter and 1 lemon slice on top of the bay leaf. Sprinkle each packet with salt, pepper and paprika. Fold foil up over fish and seal. Arrange packets in single layer 1 inch apart on baking sheet. Bake for 30 minutes. Serve one packet per person.

FISHERMEN'S MONKFISH STEW
Serves 6

2 pounds monkfish, cut into 1-inch cubes
1 cup sliced onion
1 cup celery, cut into pieces
½ cup carrots
1 8-ounce can tomato sauce
⅓ cup oil — vegetable or olive
1 teaspoon salt
½ teaspoon pepper
2 teaspoons chopped fresh parsley

In a saucepan, saute onion, carrot and celery in oil until softened. Add tomato sauce and cook for an additional three minutes, moderate heat. Add monkfish cubes, salt, pepper and parsley. Stir, lower heat and cook about 20 minutes. For more broth, add a little water. Serve with hard bread or crackers.

CATFISH IN GARLIC SAUCE
Serves 6

2 pounds catfish fillets, cut into pieces
⅓ cup olive oil
1 lemon
2 tablespoons minced garlic
2 tablespoons chopped parsley
2 teaspoons oregano
salt and pepper to taste

If desired, spray skillet with Pam. In the skillet, put oil, juice of one lemon and one teaspoon of minced garlic. Place fish in a single layer on top and let sit for a few minutes. Turn fish over and place rest of parsley, garlic, oregano, and salt and pepper. Cover, cook over medium heat for 15-20 minutes. For more juice, add a little water.

SIXTH EDITION BONUS
MORE CAPE ANN SPECIALTIES

MAURICE'S MUSSELS

"Maurice" or Tom Morris is the Director of Marketing at Empire Fish, a fresh fish company on Gloucester's Harbor Loop and has been a long-time friend of the Fishermen's Wives.

Mussels (quantity according to appetite)
White wine (Chablis preferred)
Chopped tomato, onion, and green pepper in equal quantities
Grated cheese (Swiss)
Butter—enough melted to drizzle on top
Garlic—about 1 clove, mashed
Parsley—about 2 tablespoons, chopped

Clean mussels by rinsing under cold water. Pull off threads which stick out from one side of the shell. Steam in 1 cup of water and 1 cup of wine until mussels open (approximately 8-10 minutes). Melt butter with garlic and parsley and add a little stock from the steamed mussels. Stuff mussels on their half-shell with the chopped vegetables; then sprinkle grated cheese on top. Spoon on butter mixture, and place under broiler until cheese melts.

MONKFISH PICATTA
from Blackburn Tavern

Blackburn Tavern, in Gloucester's Historic West End, is a restored Puritan House. Downstairs offers Luncheon and Dinner daily and upstairs has a large bar and weekend entertainment.

2 lbs. fresh monkfish tail	½ tsp. powdered thyme
2 cups dried bread crumbs	Salt and pepper to taste
1 cup grated parmesan cheese	2 eggs, well beaten
1 tsp. basil	1 lemon
1 tsp. chopped parsley	

Preheat oven to 350°. Remove gelatinous membrane from monkfish tail. Cut tail into medallions, about ½ inch thick. Combine bread crumbs, parmesan cheese, basil, parsley, thyme, salt and pepper. Dip fish medallions individually into egg, then dredge in crumb mixture. Place on baking dish with a small amount of water under the fish (water helps to keep the fish and crumbs moist). Lightly sprinkle with lemon juice. Bake uncovered 15-20 minutes or until fish is moist but flaky and crumbs are golden brown.

MARINATED OCTOPUS
(Lo Grasso)
from Halibut Point Restaurant

Halibut Point Restaurant, located at 289 Main Street in the original Howard Blackburn Building, is now a lively gathering spot serving Luncheons and Dinners daily.

2 pounds octopus (Portuguese)	Salt
4 fresh garlic cloves	½ celery
Fresh parsley (chopped)	4 scallions (sliced)
2 teaspoons fresh basil	½ cup oil
Ground black pepper	2 cups red wine vinegar

Poach octopus in boiling water for about 5 minutes (until it is just barely firm). Immediately remove and chill with cold water and ice. When chilled, slice legs, head and center (body) area leaving only a small area which is not edible. If sliced thin, it marinates quicker. Mix with ingredients, refrigerate 24 hours before serving. Garnish with fresh lemon and parsley.

STUFFED SOLE A LA RHUMB LINE

The Rhumb Line is located at 40 Railroad Avenue in Gloucester. They serve Luncheon daily and have a fine gourmet dining room upstairs, also serving daily. Entertainment is available on weekends.

1½ pounds fresh fillet of sole
12 mushrooms, sliced
1 garlic clove, minced
4 tablespoons butter
¼ cup chopped onion
½ pound fresh spinach, washed and dried
2 tablespoons Progresso bread crumbs
⅓ to ½ pound Swiss cheese, sliced
1 recipe hollandaise sauce

Saute mushrooms, garlic and onion in melted butter—set aside. Put fresh spinach in bottom of casserole dish and sprinkle with bread crumbs. Add 2 tablespoons of sauteed vegetables, cover with one layer of sliced Swiss cheese, put sole on top and bake 15-20 minutes at 350°F. or until bubbling. Top with hollandaise and serve.

SEVENTH EDITION BONUS
UNDERUTILIZED SPECIALTIES

STIR-FRY SKATE WITH VEGETABLES
from Gloucester on the Waterfront

Gloucester on the Waterfront, located at 17 Rogers Street, is situated amidst the city's picturesque harbors. This restaurant is dedicated to serving only fish that is fresh and uniquely prepared. Some of their specialties include the use of fresh underutilized fish, two recipes of which are described on this page.

2 pounds skate wing (filleted)
flour
3 tablespoons butter or oil
2 cloves garlic, finely chopped
2-3 fresh sprigs of parsley

juice of 2 lemons
½ cup white wine (more if needed)
vegetables: carrots, asparagus, zucchini
 red pepper, snow peas, etc.

Cut skate into long thin strips, using the cartilage indentations as a guide. Fillets 8 oz. or larger work best for this recipe (although the cartilage has been removed by filleting, you can see where they were.) Using a wok or heavy skillet, saute garlic briefly in butter or oil. Add parsley and vegetables and stir-fry for one minute; add skate (skate should be dredged in flour). Stir for 3-4 minutes, or until skate is cooked through. Deglaze with wine and stir for 15 more seconds. This recipe will go over rice or noodles very nicely. Serves 4 or more depending on how much pasta or rice is used.

STUFFED POUT WITH RICOTTA

1½ pounds pout
Cheese:
 1 pound riccotta
 1 egg
 2 tablespoons parsley
  (finely chopped)
 1 teaspoon garlic (finely chopped)
olive oil

Sauce:
 2 cups tomato puree
 1 cup white wine
 1 tablespoon garlic
  (chopped medium)
 1 tablespoon basil
 1 tablespoon shallots
 juice of 1 lemon

To make sauce, cover bottom of pan with oil, heat medium. Brown shallots and garlic, add puree, wine, basil, and lemon juice (add some water if needed). Bring to a boil and cook for about ½ hour. Mix mixture in a pastry bag. Place sauce in bottom of a baking dish, about ¼ inch deep. Wrap pout around your finger to create a shell, and place side by side on top of sauce. Fill each pout shell with cheese from pastry bag, and bake at 450° for about 15 minutes. Serves 4.

MONKFISH, SWEET N' SOUR STYLE

2 pounds monkfish tail, cut in
  1-inch chunks
2 bay leaves
½ stalk celery
½ small onion, cut in pieces
4 cups water for boiling
6 stalks celery, cut in 1-inch pieces
1½ cups green Italian olives,
  pitted and cut in pieces
3 medium-sized onions, sliced

1 can tomato paste (6 oz. can)
2 tablespoons sugar
2 medium-sized green peppers, cut in
  1-inch pieces
2 medium-sized red sweet pepper,
  cut in 1-inch pieces
1½ cups cider vinegar
½ cup vegetable oil (use as needed
  for sauteeing vegetables)

Season monkfish chunks with salt. Boil bay leaves, ½ stalk celery, and small onion for 5 minutes. Add monkfish and cook for an additional 10 minutes. Drain and place monkfish in large bowl; set aside. Discard celery, onion and bay leaves.

In large frying pan, saute the celery until tender; add to fish. Saute red and green pepper pieces; add to fish. Saute the onions for about 5 minutes; add the tomato paste, alternating with the vinegar. Mix well; add sugar and olive pieces and cook for an additional 10 minutes, stirring frequently. Season with salt and pepper. Add vegetable mixture to monkfish and refrigerate. Best when served chilled. Serves 6-8 people.

CAPT. SAM'S MARINATED FISH

Marinade: 1 cup soy sauce
         juice of 3 lemons
         1 teaspoon garlic powder
         1 teaspoon onion powder

1½ pounds monkfish or catfish
  (cut into large chunks)

seasoned bread crumbs
olive oil

Marinate fish overnight. Make sure marinade covers fish. Remove chunks of fish from marinade and lightly oil. Roll in bread crumbs. Spray a sheet of aluminum foil with a cooking spray such as Pam. Lay fish on foil and place on barbeque. Barbeque until bread crumbs are browned.

EIGHTH EDITION BONUS

The Fisherman's Wives are presently promoting underutilized species such as Cape Shark (formerly known as Dogfish—see page 13), mackerel, herring and squid, so that the other fish stocks can be replenished.

BROILED OR GRILLED MARINATED HERRING FILLETS

24 Herring fillets
2 cups seasoned bread crumbs

1½ cups red wine vinegar

Marinate the herring in red wine vinegar overnight. Dip into seasoned bread crumbs and broil or grill on medium flame approximately 5 minutes on each side.

Serve with salad.

CAPE SHARK SOUP DELIGHT

1 pound fish (Cape Shark)
½ cup diced celery
¼ cups stewed tomatoes
1 large potato cut into cubes

¼ cup olive oil
1 tablespoon parsley
½ cup diced carrots
4 cups water

In a sauce pan put onions, oil, celery, tomatoes, carrots and potato. Add 4 cups water, salt and pepper to taste. Cook for 10 minutes. Then add 2 more cups water. When it comes to a boil add the fish (cut into bite sized pieces first) and cook for 5 minutes more.

CAPE SHARK IN CRACKER CRUMBS
(a microwave fish recipe)

1 pound fillet cut into 3 or 4 pieces
mix together:
1 cup cracker crumbs (HI-HO or Ritz)
½ teaspoon parsley
dash of salt and pepper

microwave dish greased well

1 teaspoon grated cheese
¼ teaspoon garlic powder

Melt 3 tablespoons of margarine or butter and place into a small dish. Add fish. Remove coated fish and roll in the cracker mixture. Place fish in microwave dish and cover it with wax paper. Cook on high for approximately 3 minutes. Serves 3-4 people.

SQUID OVER PASTA WITH CHUNKY TOMATO BASIL SAUCE

1 pound cleaned squid cut into
  1 inch rings
¼ cup chopped fresh basil
salt and pepper to taste

4-5 cloves fresh chopped garlic
8 large ripe tomatoes
¼ cup olive oil

Saute chopped garlic in olive oil (slowly so as not to burn the garlic). Add chopped tomatoes and simmer approximately 5 minutes and then add basil, salt and pepper.

Cook spaghetti according to package directions. While spaghetti is cooking bring another pot of water to a boil and add squid rings. Cook for approximately 5 minutes (squid should be firm but not overcooked). Drain well and add tomato sauce. Place well drained pasta on a serving platter and pour sauce over it. Garnish with a sprig of fresh basil.

GERRI'S CAPE SHARK TERIYAKI

1 pound Cape Shark quartered
¼ cup sherry
4 teaspoons olive oil
grated rind of one orange

½ cup soy sauce
2 cloves garlic, crushed
½ teaspoon salt
¼ cup crushed pineapple (canned)

Combine all ingredients except Cape Shark, mix well. Add the quartered fish and marinate for one hour. Broil or barbecue. Baste with marinade while cooking. When fish flakes, it's done.

CAPE SHARK SOUP A LOVASCO

3 pounds Cape Shark cut in chunks
6 cups water
2 medium to large chopped onions
3 cups diced potatoes
¼ cup fresh chopped parsley
2 fresh ripe tomatoes or ½ cup crushed Italian tomatoes

4 cans College Inn Chicken Broth
  (13 ¾ fl. oz.)
2 cups chopped celery (use tender parts)
2 cups diced carrots
2 bay leaves

In a large pot combine broth, water and bay leaves. Bring to a boil. Add all vegetables except fish and parsley. Cook until vegetables are half cooked, then add fish, parsley and a dash of white pepper. Cook on medium heat for 15 to 20 minutes longer. Serve with garlic bread.

BAKED ZITI WITH HERRING WHITE SAUCE

2 medium onions chopped
1 small cauliflower
(cut into small pieces)
18-24 herring filets
(cut into ½ inch pieces)
¼ cup olive oil
2 envelopes saffron
1½ cups water
¼ cup toasted bread crumbs
pine nuts with golden raisins
1 cup chopped fresh fennelgreens, or 2 teaspoons crushed fennel seeds
1 pound extra thin ziti (cook according to directions)

Brown onion in olive oil, add water, saffron, cauliflower, fennel, raisins and pine nuts. Cook on medium heat 15 to 20 minutes. Add herring and cook 5 minutes longer. Drain well the cooked ziti. Mix with sauce and place in baking dish. Reserve some sauce to put on top and sprinkle with toasted bread crumbs. Bake at 350° for 15-20 minutes.

MARIE'S BAKED ZITI MELANESE (RED SAUCE)

3 cloves garlic (chopped)
1 28 oz. can crushed tomatoes
¼ cup virgin olive oil
½ cup raisins
½ cup chopped fresh fennel (greens only) or ½ teaspoon fennel seeds crushed
½ cup pine nuts
½ cup fine (toasted) bread crumbs
12-18 herring fillets (cut into ½ inch pieces)
salt and pepper to taste
1 head cauliflower cut into pieces
1 lb ziti (cook according to package directions)

In large saucepan put olive oil and garlic and lightly brown. Slowly add crushed tomatoes, fennel, cauliflower, salt, pepper, raisins and pine nuts. Cook on medium heat approximately 15 to 20 minutes. Add cut up herring fillets.

Cook ziti according to package directions. Drain well. Mix ziti with sauce (reserve a little bit for topping). Place in shallow baking dish. Top with remaining sauce. Sprinkle with toasted bread crumbs. Bake in 350° oven for 20-30 minutes.

MINTED GRILLED MACKEREL

4 mackerel (1 to 2 pounds)
4 cloves garlic (mashed in blender)
2 whole lemons (add juice to mashed garlic)
2 tablespoons olive oil
2 tablespoons minced mint (use scissors to cut fine)

Put in blender and mix above ingredients except mackerel. Take mixture and put in small bowl– (set aside). Make 3 diagonal slits on each side of mackerel. Salt and pepper to taste. Place on hot grill. Cook 5 to 6 minutes on each side (until it flakes). Baste frequently with mint mixture. Serve leftover mixture as a topping.

Serves 4-6 people.

Many thanks to Paul Newman and Joanne Woodward for these recipes.

DILLED FILETS OF SCROD Á LA NEWMAN

2 pounds scrod filets (or your favorite white fish)
3-4 tablespoons fresh dill or 1 tablespoon dried dill
½ cup (1 stick) butter   ¾ cup dry white wine
1 cup Joanne's Hollandaise Sauce (see recipe above)

Preheat oven to 375°F. Wash and dry filets. Arrange in single layer in 13"x9"x2" baking dish. Cover with fresh dill or sprinkle with dried dill. Heat butter and wine together in small saucepan until butter melts. Pour over fish. Bake for 20 minutes or just until fish separates easily when touched with a fork. Serve with Joanne's Hollandaise Sauce.

Serves 4.

JOANNE'S HOLLANDAISE SAUCE

3 egg yolks   pepper
3 tablespoons cold water   juice of ½ lemon
8 tablespoons lightly salted butter, melted

Place egg yolks and water in top of double boiler over hot but not boiling water. Stir with wooden spoon until mixture thickens. Remove from heat. Add butter, little by little, while stirring. Add pepper to taste. Just before serving, add lemon juice.

ACKNOWLEDGEMENTS

Photography	Mike Lafferty
Graphic Art	Marilyn Swift
Layout and Organization	Becky Bernie, Barbara Ericson, Lena Novello, Gerri M. Lovasco, Janis Bell, Rita Dombrowski, Mary Jo Montagnino, Eileen Matz, Rose Agrusso, Sally Davis, Patricia Davidsen, Kathy Pratl, Anita Kren, Ellie Bailey, Enid Wise, Ruth Robinson, Ann Lafferty
Technical Assistance	Dr. Perry Lane, National Marine Fisheries; Rose Agrusso, Lady Rose's Fish Market; Captain Joseph Novello
Recipes Compiled By	Grace Parsons Josie Diliberti
	Elizabeth Polizzia Margaret Favazza
	Mamie Lovasco Lena Novello
	Mary Moceri Gerri M. Lovasco

We wish to thank Mr. George Butterick, University of Connecticut for granting permission for use of the poem of Charles Olson in the book.

We also wish to thank Mr. Yon Swanson for the contribution of his poetry.

The following companies' kind donations made the publication of this cookbook possible.

Prince Macaroni Mfg. Co., of Lowell, Ma.   North Atlantic Seafoods
Blue Ribbon Fish Company of New York   Project Fish
Empire Fish Company   Oceanside Fisheries
Ocean Crest Seafoods, Inc.   Star Fisheries
The Gorton Corporation   Feener and Steiger Seafoods
O'Donnell Usen Seafoods   Arne Petersen International Inc.
Sea Pac, Division of W. R. Grace and Co.   Cape Ann Bank and Trust
Mass Coastal Seafoods, Inc.   Cape Ann Savings Bank
Lambros International   Gloucester Cooperative Bank
Seafoods International   Barbara Ericson Real Estate
All of Gloucester, Massachusetts

The Boats of the Gloucester fleet
And other organizations whose donations were received too late to be acknowledged before publication.

A special thanks to Prince Macaroni Mfg. Co. for their encouragement, enthusiasm and continued support of Mrs. Lena Novello, our number one cook.

94

Lobster or crab or haddock or sole,
Succulent shrimp or a fish chowder bowl,
Tart lemony baked fish or fried oyster plate,
To this kind of dining, no one comes late.

The best of our recipes here offered to you,
With the bonus surprise — they're not hard to do.
Taste fork tender sea food — pitch out your knives,
Who better to learn from than fishermen's wives?

O. Kay Jackson

INDEX OF RECIPES
Special Edition Bonus Sections contain
recipes not indexed. Check them out!

The Gloucester Fishermen's Wives Memorial
Sculpture by Morgan Faulds Pike
Dedicated 2001

The Gloucester Fishermen's Wives Association:
A Brief History of the Organization's Advocacy Work

Since its founding in 1969, the Gloucester Fishermen's Wives Association has been a powerful voice representing the interests of fishermen, serving to promote the New England fishing industry, preserve the Atlantic Ocean as a sustainable food supply for the world, and assist active and retired fishermen and their families to live better lives. In the early years, a group of fishermen's wives that would later formally organize to become the GFWA came together to combat foreign factory trawlers in U.S. waters, ultimately achieving success with the establishment of a 200-mile exclusive economic zone. Also in the early days, the GFWA worked to educate the public and promote underutilized species from our waters, achieving success in this effort with the publication of the first edition of *The Taste of Gloucester* in collaboration with the League of Women Voters.

In later years the organization gained momentum and public support, expanding its focus to mount successful campaigns including the prevention of oil drilling on Georges Bank, terminating the practice of ocean dumping in local waters, halting the development of a tire reef outside of Gloucester Harbor, and establishing the National Marine Sanctuary on Stellwagen Bank. The organization has also fought hard over the years to advocate for fair and equal regulations, continuously supported collaborative research projects and participated in countless public and private planning initiatives. More recently, the GFWA helped found the Massachusetts Fishermens Partnership, an organization of commercial fishing organizations that works to provide solutions to problems common to all fishermen.

For over thirty years, the GFWA has provided fishermen and their families with the resources and assistance needed to live healthy and successful lives. They have worked with the Fishing Partnership Health Plan to provide affordable healthcare, offered safety trainings in collaboration with the U.S. Coast Guard, and provided job training and captains licensing programs. In times of great need, the Wives have consistently opened their homes and their hearts to members of the fishing community. In 1998, the Wives created a narrative quilt to commemorate and honor the history and faith of the fishing industry. In 2001, the GFWA dedicated a memorial to honor the women who are the soul of fishing communities. The eight foot bronze sculpture overlooking Gloucester Harbor serves as a testimonial to what wives, mothers, sisters, and children of fishermen of the world have endured because their men chose to be on the water. Later, in 2005, the

GFWA published a second cookbook called *Gloucester Fishermen's Wives Cookbook: Stories and Recipes* which highlights the stories of fourteen fishermen's wives and shares their family recipes.

The GFWA's work is far from over. An increasingly restrictive regulatory environment, rising business costs and a shrinking fleet have meant that local fishermen need support now more than ever. The GFWA's newest initiative-- Cape Ann Fresh Catch (CAFC)— was conceived and designed with the main purpose of alleviating some of the hardships faced by small-scale, economically disadvantaged fishermen. Ultimately this initiative hopes to breathe new life into the industry by opening up new marketing opportunities for fishermen, guaranteeing them a fair price for their catch, and promoting sustainable fishing practices, all while reconnecting consumers with their local food producers. Looking forward, the GFWA will continue to fight for fair and just regulations that protect our oceans and ensure the preservation and health of local fishing communities throughout the world.

The League marches for the Equal Rights Ammendment in the 1976 Horribles Parade.

The League of Women Voters of Cape Ann

The League of Women Voters was founded in 1920 as soon as women won the right to vote. Our purpose is to make the political process accessible to all voters, men and women, new citizens, young and old, and to improve the lives and welfare of residents of our community through public action. During the McCarthy Era the League was a beacon for freedom of speech and due process under law, and an opponent of politics by innuendo and smear. Our Cape Ann League has existed in its present form since 1967.

We are non-partisan: the League never supports individual candidates for public office or the platform of any political party; we study and evaluate each issue on its own merits before deciding to support or oppose. LWVCA has conducted studies on local government, state finance, education, School Choice, welfare laws, birth control and abortion, housing, harbor proposals, domestic violence, health care, drinking water, open space and juvenile justice.

The League is known for its work in registering new voters and explaining how the election process works. We sponsor debates for key local races, serve as volunteer poll workers on Election Day, and provide in-depth information to voters about referendum questions.

The LWVCA is concerned with environmental issues. We've sponsored Fairs about safer alternatives to toxic lawn and garden products and actively lobbied in support of environmental legislation and public health.

The League monitors the performance of our local government, for example, adherence to the Open Meeting Law, and guaranteeing citizen's access to public information. In the 1990's we produced *"Spotlight on City Hall"* – a video about Gloucester's various public offices.

The Katherine T. Nutbrown Scholarship, named for a long time member whose life and work inspired all of us, is a $500 award given annually by the League to a graduating senior from *each* of Cape Ann's high schools, in recognition of scholarship, need and community service.

As a non-partisan organization we assume that no position is absolute, that compromise is always possible, and that no group should be shut out of the public discourse by "winner-take-all" strategies. We believe a grass roots organization is best way to combat the influence of money on the political agenda. We believe that unbiased, factual information presented by an organization of unimpeachable integrity can overcome the reduction of complex issues to slogans and negative ads.

Our relationship with the Gloucester Fishermen's Wives Association has been one of the most satisfying of the many partnerships the League forms with other community groups. The proceeds from sales of *The Taste of Gloucester Cookbook* support all our voter services and other activities.